FRENCH FOR YOUR POCKET

A Headway phrasebook

Ena Fowler

Headway · Hodder & Stoughton

© 1990 Ena Fowler

First published in Great Britain 1990

Third impression 1992

British Library Cataloguing in Publication Data
Fowler, Ena
  French in your pocket.—(In your pocket)
  1. French language.
  I. Title
  448

ISBN 0 340 50913 9

Typeset by Wearside Tradespools, Fulwell, Sunderland
Printed and bound in Hong Kong for Hodder and Stoughton
Limited, Mill Road, Dunton Green, Sevenoaks, Kent by
Colorcraft Ltd.

Contents

Introduction

If you know very little French, or need to brush up what you once knew, *French in your pocket* is for you. It covers the situations you are most likely to meet on a holiday or short journey abroad, from the first confusion of arrival at a main-line railway station, to dealing with Customs as a seasoned traveller on your return.

In addition to the vocabulary, some hints and addresses have been included to provide practical help. The Contents list makes it easy to find the words for the particular situation you are in, while the general vocabulary at the end is handy for reference.

The words in italics below each phrase are a guide to the actual sound of the words, which is sometimes quite different from what we would expect from the spelling. The key to this is on page 5. If you can find a native French speaker to read the key aloud, you will soon get a good idea of the pronunciation. It would be a good idea to study the pronunciation (page 5) and the basic expressions (page 6) before starting on the book itself.

Don't be discouraged if at first you forget what you thought you had learnt the day before. To learn ten words a day thoroughly is a worthwhile achievement. Before long you will find that through repeated use, the words are becoming unforgettable.

Bon voyage, and *bonne chance!*

Pronunciation guide

symbol		French word		English word
a	*as in*	salle	*compare with*	family
ay		marché		faded
e		le		other
ee		il		eel
eh		est		men
eh-y		soleil		very (without the 'r')
er		deux		purr (without the 'r')
err		heure		purr (with the 'r')
ew		tu		see below
e-y		feuille		furry (without the 'r')
j		je		pleasure
o		solide		pot
oh		trop		wrote
sh		chien		shoot
s		ici		cereal
k		canard		cook

nasals

ahŋ	sans	**uŋ**	**un**
aŋ	medecin	**yaŋ**	**bien**
oŋ	carton		

- French words do not have very pronounced stresses. If there is a stress, it is normally on the last syllable.
- The sound **ew**, as in 'tu', is not pronounced like the English 'few', but is more like an **ee** sound spoken with the lips in the position for **oo**.
- **e-y** is a two-part sound: combine the **e** from 'other' with the **ee** from 'me'.
- **ay** and **oh** are *not* two-part sounds. They are pronounced as short, simple sounds, without the final 'ee' or 'oo' they have in English.
- French 'r' is always strongly pronounced at the back of the mouth. Therefore 'car' (='because' in French) is not pronounced the same way as the English word 'car', where the 'r' is hardly heard, but as 'ca+r'.
- Finally, there are several nasal sounds in French: these are characterised by the presence of an 'n' (ŋ) which is not sounded like the 'n' in English 'can', but more like the 'n' in English 'singing'.

Basic expressions

yes	oui *wee*
no	non *noŋ*
please	s'il vous plaît *seel voo pleh*
thank you	merci *mehrsee*
sorry	pardon/excusez-moi *pardoŋ/ehxkewzay mwa*
pardon?	pardon? *pardoŋ?*
hello	bonjour *boŋjoor*
how are you?	comment allez-vous? *komahŋt alay voo?*
goodbye	au revoir *oh rvwar*
help!	au secours! *oh skoor!*
I am ill	Je suis malade *jswee malad*
How much is it?	C'est combien? *seh koŋbyaŋ?*
What does that mean?	Qu'est-ce que ça veut dire? *kehske sa ver deer?*
I don't know	Je ne sais pas *je ne seh pah*
Good morning	Bonjour *boŋjoor*
Good afternoon	Bonjour *Boŋjoor*
Good evening	Bonsoir *boŋswar*
Good night	Bonne nuit *bon nwee*

Basic expressions

I don't speak French	Je ne parle pas français *je ne parl pah frahŋseh*
Could you speak more slowly?	Pouvez-vous parler plus lentement? *poovay voo parlay plew lahŋtmahŋ?*
I don't understand	Je n'ai pas compris *jnay pah koŋpree*
Do you speak English?	Parlez-vous anglais? *parlay vooz ahŋgleh?*
Where are the toilets?	Où sont les toilettes s'il vous plaît monsieur/madame/mademoiselle? *oo soŋ lay twaleht seel voo pleh msyer, madam, madmwazehl?*
Can you help me?	Pouvez-vous m'aider, s'il vous plaît? *poovay voo mehday seel voo pleh?*
it's	c'est *seh*
it's not	ce n'est pas *sneh pah*
What is it?	Qu'est-ce que c'est? *kehskeseh?*
good	bon *boŋ*
bad	mauvais *mohveh*
more	plus *plew*
less	moins *mwaŋ*
better	mieux *myer*
worse	pire *peer*

too	trop
	troh
where	où
	oo
when	quand
	kahŋ
how	comment
	komahŋ
must I/we/one . . . ?	faut-il . . . ?
	fohteel . . . ?
can I/we/one . . . ?	peut-on . . . ?
	pertohŋ . . . ?
will you	voulez-vous
	voolay-voo
I'd like	je voudrais
	je voodreh
these	ceux-ci
	sersee
those	ceux-là
	serla

- It is important to add *s'il vous plaît, merci, monsieur, madame* or *mademoiselle* to your enquiries; not to do so seems much ruder in French than in English.
- Use of *tu* or *vous*: as a general rule, *tu* is used when speaking to relatives, close friends and children. Teenagers and students use *tu* among themselves. *Vous* is used elsewhere. It is not polite to use *tu* to an adult stranger or a shopkeeper.
- *Merci* on its own in reply to a question such as 'Would you like some tea?' means '*No* thank you', so say '*Oui*, merci' if you would like some.

ARRIVAL AND DEPARTURE

- At the Paris airports you can buy a *billet de tourisme* for cut-price travel; see page 95 for alternatives.
- At the main-line railway stations you will be able to find the *hôtesses de Paris*, who will provide you with help and information, and telephone around for a hotel vacancy for you.
- It is not always an easy task to reach your hotel by Metro (underground). If you get a (free) map of the bus routes (*une carte du réseau*) from the information bureau, you may find a bus route to take you straight there.
- If you take a taxi, the usual tip is 10% to 15%.
- For your return home, you will find up-to-date leaflets at the duty-free shops at ports and airports, listing the amounts of alcohol, perfume, etc. which may be taken home duty-free.

Asking the way

Excuse me, where is . . . ?	Excusez-moi, où est . . . ? *ehxkewzay mwa, oo eh . . . ?*
. . . the bar	. . . le bar *le bar*
. . . the car hire	. . . l'agence de location de voitures *lajahŋs de lokasyoŋ de vwatewr*
. . . the car park	. . . le parking *le parkeeng*
. . . the exchange bureau	. . . le bureau de change *le bewroh de shahŋj*
. . . the exit	. . . la sortie *la sortee*
. . . the information bureau	. . . le syndicat d'initiative *le saŋdeeka deeneesyateev*
	. . . le bureau de renseignements *le bewroh de rahŋsehnyemahŋ*
. . . the left-luggage office (baggage check)	. . . la consigne *la koŋseenye*
. . . the Metro	. . . le Métro *le maytroh*
. . . the restaurant	. . . le restaurant *le restohrahŋ*
. . . the waiting room	. . . la salle d'attente *la sal datahŋt*
. . . the ticket office	. . . le guichet *le geesheh*
. . . the bus stop	. . . l'arrêt d'autobus *lareh dohtobews*

Excuse me, where are the . . . ?	Excusez-moi, où sont les . . . ? *ehxkewzay mwa, oo son lay . . . ?*
. . . taxis	. . . taxis *taxee*
. . . toilets	. . . toilettes *twaleht*

Where can I . . . ?	Où est-ce que je peux . . . ? *oo ehske je per . . . ?*
. . . find my luggage	. . . trouver mes bagages *troovay may bagaj*
. . . find a porter	. . . trouver un porteur *troovay un porterr*
. . . get a taxi	. . . prendre un taxi *prahndr un taxee*

How do I get to . . . ?	Pour aller à . . . ? *poor alay a . . . ?*
How far away is the . . . ?	Le/la . . . est à quelle distance? *le/la . . . ehta kel deestahns?*
Is there a bus stop near here?	Y a-t-il un arrêt d'autobus près d'ici? *yateel un areh dohtobews preh deesee?*
Is it far?	Est-ce loin? *ehs lwan?*
Is it near?	Est-ce près? *ehs preh?*
Where's the nearest . . . ?	Où est le/la . . . le/la plus proche? *oo eh le/la . . . le/la plew prosh?*

Could you repeat that, please?

Voulez-vous répéter, s'il vous plaît?
voolay voo raypaytay, seel voo pleh?

Could you speak more slowly?

Voulez-vous parler plus lentement?
voolay voo parlay plew lahntmahŋ?

I didn't understand.

Je n'ai pas compris
jnay pah koŋpree

You may hear:

Prenez...
Prenay...

Take...

...la première rue
la premyehr rew

...the first street

...la deuxième rue
la derzyehm rew

...the second street

...à droite
a drwat

...on the right

...à gauche
a gohsh

...on the left

Allez tout droit
alay too drwa

Go straight on

Il faut...
eel foh...

You have to...

...tourner à droite
toornay a drwat

...turn right

...tourner à gauche
toornay a gohsh

...turn left

au bout de la rue
oh boo de la rew

at the end of the street

Il/elle est à deux kilomètres, à peu près
eel/ehl eht a der keelohmetr, a per preh

It's about two kilometres away

Getting a porter

Porter!	Porteur! *porterr!*
Will you take . . . ?	Voulez-vous prendre . . . ? *voolay-voo prahŋdr . . . ?*
. . . all that	. . . tout ça *too sa*
. . . my luggage	. . . mes bagages *may bagaj*
. . . my suitcase	. . . ma valise *ma valeez*
. . . my suitcases	. . . mes valises *may valeez*
Could you take it/them . . .	Voulez-vous l'/les apporter . . . *voolay voo laportay/ layzaportay . . .*
. . . to the exit	. . . à la sortie *a la sortee*
. . . to the luggage lockers	. . . à la consigne automatique *a la koŋseenye ohtomateek*
. . . to platform number 2	. . . à la voie numéro 2 *a la vwa newmayroh der*
. . . to the restaurant	. . . au restaurant *oh rehstohrahŋ*
. . . to the taxi rank	. . . à la station de taxis *a la stasyoŋ de taxee*
There's a suitcase missing	Il manque une valise *eel mahŋk ewn valeez*

Getting a taxi

Where can I get a taxi?	Où est-ce que je peux trouver un taxi? *oo ehske je per troovay uŋ taxee?*
I want to go to . . .	Je veux aller à . . . *je ver alay a . . .*
. . . this address	. . . cette adresse *seht adrehs*
. . . the airport	. . . l'aéroport *la-ayropor*
. . . the bus station	. . . la gare routière *la gar rootyehr*
. . . the railway station	. . . la gare *la gar*
Not so fast, please!	Moins vite, s'il vous plaît! *mwaŋ veet, seel voo pleh!*
Stop here, please	Arrêtez-vous ici, s'il vous plaît *arehtay voo eesee, seel voo pleh*
Will you wait for me, please?	Voulez-vous m'attendre, s'il vous plaît? *voolay voo matahŋdr, seel voo pleh?*
How much is it?	C'est combien? *seh koŋbyaŋ?*
Here's something for you (a tip)	Voici pour vous *vwasee poor voo*
I'm in a hurry	Je suis pressé(e) *jswee prehsay*
Could you help me with my luggage?	Pouvez-vouz m'aider à porter mes bagages? *poovay voo mehday a portay may bagaj?*

At the customs

I'm British	Je suis britannique *je swee breetaneek*
I'm American	Je suis américain/e *je swee amayreekaŋ/* *amayreekehn*
Here it (they) is (are)	Le (les) voici *le (lay) vwasee*
I don't know	Je ne sais pas *je ne seh pah*
I don't understand	Je ne comprends pas *je ne koŋprahŋ pah*

I've bought . . .	J'ai acheté . . . *jay ashtay . . .*

. . . a carton of cigarettes	. . . une cartouche de cigarettes *ewn kartoosh de seegareht*
. . . a bottle of . . .	. . . une bouteille de . . . *ewn booteh-y de . . .*
. . . a film	. . . une pellicule *ewn pehleekewl*
. . . some souvenirs	. . . des souvenirs *day soovneer*
. . . a watch	. . . une montre *ewn moŋtr*
. . . some perfume	. . . du parfum *dew parfuŋ*

It's for my personal use	C'est pour mon usage personnel *seh poor mon ewzaj pehrsonehl*

15

You may hear:

Votre passeport, s'il vous plaît *votr paspor seel voo pleh*	May I see your passport, please?
Vous vous appelez comment? *voo voozapelay komaŋ?*	What's your name?
Vous êtes de quelle nationalité? *voozeht de kehl nasyonaleetay?*	What nationality are you?
Vous allez rester combien de temps? *vooz alay rehstay kombyaŋ de tahŋ?*	How long are you staying?
Montrez-moi vos bagages, s'il vous plaît *montray mwa voh bagaj seel voo pleh*	Show me your luggage, please
Qu'est-ce que vous avez acheté en France? *kehske vooz avay ashtay aŋ fraŋs?*	What have you bought in France?
Où l'avez-vous acheté(e)? *oo lavay voo ashtay?*	Where did you buy it?
Quand l'avez-vous acheté(e)? *koŋ lavay voo ashtay?*	When did you buy it?
Il/elle a coûté combien? *eel/ehl a kootay koŋbyaŋ?*	How much did it cost?
Je regrette, il faut payer les droits de douane *je regreht, eel foh payay lay drwa de dooan*	I'm sorry, you'll have to pay duty
Vous n'avez rien à déclarer? *voo navay ryaŋ a dayklaray?*	Haven't you anything to declare?
Avez-vous d'autres bagages? *avay voo dohtr bagaj?*	Have you any other luggage?

ACCOMMODATION

- Lists of campsites and youth hostels can be obtained from the French Tourist Office at 127 Champs-Elysées, Paris, and at the main railway stations.
- Camping in France provides a comparatively inexpensive way to see the country, and the sites are usually very well organised. Off-site camping is not always allowed (look out for *camping interdit* signs).
- Official camp sites have a star rating, according to amenities. You usually have to pay separately for the plot, the vehicle, electricity and showers.
- When youth hostelling, you will be asked for your YHA card and passport when you arrive.
- If you are without accommodation on arrival in a strange town, you will find a list at the local information office (*Syndicat d'Initiative*). The hotels are given star ratings according to their amenities. You should ask whether or not breakfast and showers are included in the price.

- Cheaper (but charming, clean and comfortable) accommodation is often available at *pensions* (boarding houses), *auberges* and *logis de France*. Don't confuse *auberges* (country inns) with *auberges de jeunesse* (youth hostels).
- When you register at a hotel, boarding house or campsite, you will be asked to fill a registration form (*une fiche*) and to hand over your passport, which will be returned to you after the details have been taken.

You may see:

Nom/Prénom	Surname/first name
Lieu de domicile/rue/n°	Address/Street/No
Date/lieu de naissance	Date/place of birth
Numéro de passeport	Passport number
Lieu/Date	Place/date
Signature	Signature

Is there a hotel near here?	Est-ce qu'il y a un hôtel près d'ici? *ehskeelya un ohtehl preh deesee?*
My name is . . .	Je m'appelle . . . *jmapehl . . .*
I have a reservation	J'ai réservé *jay rayzehrvay*
Where is the the nearest campsite?	Où se trouve le camping le plus proche? *oo se troov le kahŋpeeŋ le plew prosh?*
Is it expensive?	C'est cher? *seh shehr?*
We're staying for one night	On va rester une nuit *on va restay ewn nwee*
There are two of us	Nous sommes deux *noo som der*

Camping

I'd like to hire . . .	Je voudrais louer . . . *je voodreh looay . . .*
Have you . . . ?	Avez-vous . . . ? *avay voo . . . ?*
How much does . . . cost?	C'est combien pour . . . ? *seh koŋbyaŋ poor . . . ?*
I have booked	J'ai réservé *jay rayzehrvay*
I haven't booked	Je n'ai pas réservé *jnay pah rayzehrvay*
a bed	un lit *uŋ lee*
a blanket	une couverture *ewn koovehrtewr*
a car	une voiture *ewn vwatewr*
a caravan	une caravane *ewn karavan*
electricity	l'électricité *laylehktreeseetay*
one person	une personne *ewn pehrson*
sheets	des draps *day dra*
a shower	une douche *ewn doosh*
a sleeping bag	un sac de couchage *uŋ sak de kooshaj*
a site	un emplacement *uŋ ahŋplasmahŋ*
a tent	une tente *ewn tahnt*
youth hostel	une auberge de jeunesse *ewn ohbehrj de jernehs*

19

for one night	pour une nuit *poor ewn nwee*
for two nights	pour deux nuits *poor der nwee*
for a week	pour une semaine *poor ewn smehn*

Where is/are . . .	Où est/sont . . . *oo eh/soŋ . . .*

. . . the bar	. . . le bar *le bar*
. . . the dormitory	. . . le dortoir *le dortwar*
. . . the car park	. . . le parking *le parkeeng*
. . . the food store	. . . l'alimentation *laleemahŋtasyoŋ*
. . . the launderette	. . . la laverie *la lavree*
. . . the pancake parlour	. . . la crêperie *la krehpree*
. . . the reception office	. . . le bureau d'acceuil *le bewroh dak-e-y*
. . . the restaurant	. . . le restaurant *le rehstohrahŋ*
. . . the self-service	. . . le libre-service *le leebr sehrvees*
. . . the snack bar	. . . le snack *le snak*
. . . the showers	. . . les douches *lay doosh*
. . . the toilets	. . . les toilettes *lay twaleht*

Accommodation

Can you lend me . . .	Pouvez-vous me prêter . . .
	poovay voo me prehtay . . .
. . . a corkscrew	. . . un tire-bouchon
	uŋ teer booshoŋ
. . . a frying pan	. . . une poêle
	ewn pwal
. . . a knife	. . . un couteau
	uŋ kootoh
. . . some matches	. . . des allumettes
	dayz alewmeht
. . . a saucepan	. . . une casserole
	ewn kassrol
. . . a spoon	. . . une cuillère
	ewn kweeyehr
. . . a tin opener	. . . un ouvre-boîte
	uŋ oovr bwat

There isn't any hot water	Il n'y a pas d'eau chaude
	eel nya pah doh shohd
There aren't any matches	Il n'y a pas d'allumettes
	eel nya pah dalewmeht
The light isn't working	La lumière ne fonctionne pas
	la lewmyehr ne foŋkseeyon pah
the plug/socket	la prise
	la preez
the tap (faucet)	le robinet
	le robeenay
The toilet is blocked	Le WC est bouché
	le vaysay eh booshay
The window is jammed	La fenêtre est coincée
	la fenehtr eh kwaŋsay

Extra vocabulary

air bed/lilo	le matelas pneumatique *le matla pnermateek*
camp site	le camping/le terrain *le kahŋpeeŋ/le tehraŋ*
floor/storey	un étage *uŋ aytaj*
camping gas	le gaz *le gaz*
cooker	la cuisinière *la kweezeenyehr*
dormitory	le dortoir *le dortwar*
drinking water	l'eau potable (f) *loh potabl*
dustbin (garbage can)	la poubelle *la poobehl*
lamp/light/torch	la lampe *la lahŋp*
plug (in a sink)	le tampon *le taŋpoŋ*
plug/ power point	la prise *la preez*
rucksack	le sac à dos *le sak a doh*
rules/regulations	le règlement *le rehglmahŋ*
shower block	le block sanitaire *le blok saneetehr*
sleeping bag	le sac de couchage *le sak de kooshaj*
supplement/ extra charge	le supplément *le sewplaymahŋ*
warden	le gardien *le gardyaŋ*

At a hotel

Have you any rooms?	Avez-vous des chambres? *avay voo day shahmbr?*
No, I haven't booked	Non, je n'ai pas réservé *non, jnay pah raysehrvay*
I'd like to book a room	Je voudrais réserver une chambre *je voodreh rayservay ewn shanbr*

What is the cost of a room . . . ?	Quel est le prix d'une chambre . . . ? *kehl eh le pree dewn shanbr . . . ?*
. . . for one	. . . pour une personne *poor ewn pehrson*
. . . for two	. . . pour deux personnes *poor der pehrson*
. . . for a family	. . . de famille *de famee*
. . . with one bed	. . . avec un lit *avehk un lee*
. . . with a double bed	. . . avec grand lit *avehk gran lee*
. . . with two beds	. . . avec deux lits *avehk der lee*
. . . with an extra bed	. . . avec lit supplémentaire *avehk lee sewplaymahntehr*
. . . with a shower	. . . avec douche *avehk doosh*
. . . without a shower	. . . sans douche *sahn doosh*
. . . with a bathroom	. . . aevec salle de bains *avehk sal de ban*

23

. . . without a bathroom	. . . sans salle de bains *sahŋ sal de baŋ*
. . . with a toilet	. . . avec WC *avehk vay say*

Our party consists of two adults and three children	Nous sommes deux adultes et trois enfants *noo som derz adewlt ay trwaz ahŋfahŋ*

How much is it . . . ?	C'est combien . . . ? *seh koŋbyan . . . ?*
. . . per day	. . . par jour *par joor*
. . . per person	. . . par personne *par pehrson*
. . . per night	. . . par nuit *par nwee*
. . . weekly	. . . par semaine *par smehn*
. . . for half-board	. . . la demi-pension *la dmee pahŋsyoŋ*
. . . for full board	. . . la pension complète *la pahŋsyoŋ koŋpleht*

Is breakfast included?	Le petit déjeuner est compris? *le ptee dayjernay eh koŋpree?*
Are tax and service included?	Taxes et service compris? *tax ay sehrvees koŋpree?*
Is there a reduced rate for children?	Y a-t-il un tarif réduit pour les enfants? *yateel uŋ tareef raydwee poor layz ahŋfahŋ?*
What floor is the room on?	La chambre est à quel étage? *la shahŋbr ehta kehlaytaj?*

Accommodation

on the ground floor	au rez-de-chaussée *oh ray de shohsay*
on the second floor	au deuxième étage *oh derzyehm aytaj*
on the third floor	au troisième étage *oh trwazyehm aytaj*
on the fourth floor	au quatrième étage *oh katryehm aytaj*
Is there a lift (elevator)?	Y a-t-il un ascenseur? *yateel uŋ assahŋserr?*
It's too expensive	C'est trop cher *seh troh shehr*
Have you anything cheaper?	Avez-vous quelque chose de moins cher? *avay voo kehlkeshohz de mwaŋ shehr?*
We'll take them, please	On les prend, s'il vous plaît *oŋ lay prahŋ, seel voo pleh*
We are leaving on Sunday	On part dimanche *oŋ par deemahŋsh*
Do you want a deposit?	Voulez-vous une caution? *voolay voo ewn kohsyoŋ?*
Do you want to see our passports?	Voulez-vous voir nos passeports? *voolay voo vwar noh paspor?*
At what time do you . . . ?	A quelle heure est-ce qu'on . . . ? *a kehl err ehskoŋ . . . ?*
. . . have breakfast	. . . prend le petit déjeuner *prahŋ le ptee dayjernay*
. . . have lunch	. . . déjeune *dayjern*
. . . dine	. . . dîne *deen*

25

How far away is . . . ?	. . . est à quelle distance? *ehta kehl deestahŋs?*
. . . the beach	La plage . . . *la plaj . . .*
. . . the railway station	La gare . . . *la gar . . .*
. . . the centre of town	Le centre-ville . . . *le sahŋtrveel . . .*
May I have . . .	Voulez-vous me donner . . . *voolay voo me donay . . .*
. . . the bill (the check)	. . . la note *la not*
. . . a key	. . . une clef *ewn klay*
. . . an extra pillow	. . . un oreiller supplémentaire *uŋ orehyay* *sewplaymahŋtehr*
. . . some soap	. . . du savon *dew savoŋ*
. . . a towel	. . . une serviette *ewn sehrvyeht*
. . . an ashtray	. . . un cendrier *uŋ sahŋdreeay*
. . . an extra blanket	. . . une couverture supplémentaire *ewn koovehrtewr* *sewplaymahŋtehr*
. . . some writing paper	. . . du papier à lettres *dew papyay a lehtr*
. . . some toilet paper	. . . du papier hygiénique *dew papyay eejyayneek*
I haven't got one/any	Je n'en ai pas *jnahŋ ay pah*

Accommodation

Extra vocabulary

basement	le sous-sol *le soo sol*
deposit	la caution *la kohsyoŋ*
form	la fiche *la feesh*
ground floor	le rez-de-chaussée *le ray de shohsay*
lift (elevator)	un ascenseur *uŋ assahŋserr*
luggage	les bagages *lay bagaj*
to pay the bill (check)	régler la note *rayglay la not*
payment	le règlement *le rehglmahŋ*
staircase	un escalier *uŋ ehskalyay*
telephone	le téléphone *le taylayfon*
washbasin	le lavabo *le lavaboh*
bathroom	la salle de bains *la sal de baŋ*
light bulb	une ampoule *ewn aŋpool*
maid	la femme de chambre *la fam de shahŋbr*
safe	le coffre-fort *le koffr for*
garage	le garage *le garaj*
manager	le propriétaire *le propreeaytehr*

You may hear:

Vous avez réservé?
vooz avay raysehrvay?

Have you booked?

Vous avez des pièces d'identité?
vooz avay day pyehs deedahŋteetay?

Have you any identification?

Les repas ne sont pas compris
lay repah ne soŋ pah koŋpree

Meals are not included

Il n'y a pas d'ascenseur
eel nya pah dassahŋserr

There isn't a lift (elevator)

Voulez-vous remplir cette fiche?
voolay voo rahŋpleer set feesh?

Would you fill in this form?

Signez ici, s'il vous plaît
seenyay eesee seel voo pleh

Sign here, please

Vous restez combien de nuits?
voo restay koŋbyaŋ de nwee?

How long are you staying?

Il n'y a pas de place
eel nya pah de plas

There is no room

Could you bring breakfast to my room?

Pouvez-vous m'apporter le petit déjeuner dans ma chambre?
poovay voo maportay le ptee dayjernay daŋ ma shahŋbr?

Could you call me at 7 o'clock?

Pouvez-vous m'appeler à sept heures?
poovay voo maplay a set err?

Do you have foreign newspapers?

Avez-vous des journaux étrangers?
avay voo day joornoh aytrahŋjay?

Apartments

I would like an apartment . . .	Je voudrais un appartement . . . *je voodreh uŋ apartemahŋ . . .*
. . . with one bedroom	. . . avec une chambre *avehk ewn shahŋbr*
. . . with two bedrooms	. . . avec deux chambres *avehk der shahŋbr*
. . . with a bathroom	. . . avec salle de bains *avehk sal de baŋ*
. . . for two people	. . . pour deux personnes *poor der pehrson*
. . . for a week	. . . pour une semaine *poor ewn smehn*
. . . for a fortnight	. . . pour quinze jours *poor kaŋz joor*
. . . with a balcony	. . . avec balcon *avehk balkoŋ*
. . . with a swimming pool	. . . avec piscine *avehk peeseen*

Which floor is it on?	C'est à quel étage? *seht a kehl aytaj?*
I prefer the first/ground floor	Je préfère le premier étage/le rez de chaussée *je prayfehr le premyehr aytaj/ le ray de shohsay*
How many beds are there?	Combien de lits y a-t-il? *koŋbyaŋ de lee yateel?*
How many bedrooms are there?	Combien de chambres y a-t-il? *koŋbyaŋ de shahŋbr yateel?*
Is there a sofa-bed?	Est-ce qu'il y a un canapé-lit? *ehskeelya uŋ kanapay lee?*

Is . . . included?	Est-ce que . . . est compris? *ehske . . . eh koŋpree?*
. . . everything	. . . tout *toot*
. . . the gas	. . . le gaz *le gaz*
. . . the electricity	. . . l'électricité *laylehktreeseetay*
. . . the rubbish collection	. . . le ramassage d'ordures *le ramasaj dordewr*
. . . the cleaning	. . . le nettoyage *le nethtwayaj*
Is there a receptionist/ caretaker?	Y a-t-il un réceptionniste/ concierge? *yateel uŋ raysehpsyoneest/ koŋsyehrj?*
When . . . ?	Quand . . . ? *kahŋt . . . ?*
. . . is it cleaned	. . . est-ce qu'on le nettoie *ehskoŋ le nehtwa*
. . . are the sheets changed	. . . est-ce qu'on change les draps *ehskoŋ shahŋj lay dra*
. . . is the pool cleaned	. . . est-ce qu'on nettoie la piscine *ehskoŋ nehtwa la peeseen*

| I need . . . | J'ai besoin d'un . . . |
| | *jay bezwaŋ duŋ . . .* |

| . . . a plumber | . . . plombier |
| | *ploŋbyay* |

| . . . an electrician | . . . électricien |
| | *aylehktreesyaŋ* |

| . . . a gas worker | . . . employé du GDF |
| | *ahŋplwayay dew jay day ehf* |

| Does it have . . . ? | Y a-t-il . . . ? |
| | *yateel . . . ?* |

| . . . an oven | . . . un four |
| | *uŋ foor* |

| . . . a grill | . . . un gril |
| | *uŋ greel* |

| . . . central heating | . . . chauffage central |
| | *shohfaj sahŋtral* |

| . . . air conditioning | . . . climatisation |
| | *kleemateezasyoŋ* |

| . . . a fridge | . . . un frigo |
| | *un freegoh* |

| . . . a TV | . . . une télévision |
| | *ewn taylayvizyoŋ* |

| . . . a washing machine | . . . une machine à laver |
| | *ewn masheen a lavay* |

| Is it electric or gas? | Y a-t-il l'électricité ou le gaz? |
| | *yateel laylehktreeseetay oo le gaz?see* |

Checking out

May I have the bill (check), please?	L'addition, s'il vous plaît *ladisyoŋ seel voo pleh*
Is everything included?	Tout est compris? *toot eh koŋpree?*
Can I pay by credit card?	Puis-je payer avec une carte de crédit? *pweej payay avehk ewn kart de kraydee?*
Can you get us a taxi?	Pouvez-vous nous appeler un taxi? *poovay voo nooz aplay uŋ taxee?*
Could somebody bring down our luggage?	Est-ce que quelqu'un pourrait descendre nos bagages? *ehske kehlkuŋ pooreh daysahŋdr noh bagaj?*
Here's the forwarding address	Faites suivre le courrier à cette adresse *feht sweevr le kooryay a seht adrehs*
Could we have our passports, please?	Pourriez-vous nous rendre nos passeports? *pooryay voo noo rahŋdr noh passpor?*
I must leave immediately	Il faut que je parte tout de suite *eel foh ke je part toot sweet*
How much were the telephone calls?	À combien se monte ma note de téléphone? *a koŋbyaŋ se moŋt ma not de taylayfon?*
I think there's a mistake on the bill	Je crois qu'il y a erreur sur la note *je krwa keelya ehrerr sewr la not*
You've charged too much	Vous m'avez trop compté sur la note *voo mavay troh koŋtay sewr la not*

EATING OUT

- Some meals, as well as the usual coffee and drinks, are obtainable at bars, *bistrots*, snack bars and cafés. Prices are often more expensive at the tables than at the bar, and even more expensive outside on the verandah.
- *Salons de thé* specialize in pastries, ice cream and tea or coffee. Meals are occasionally served.
- Full meals are found in railway station buffets (often surprisingly good), *brasseries*, *routiers*, *restoroutes* and *auberges*.
- The most expensive meals are served in *hostelleries*, *relais de campagne*, *rôtisseries* and restaurants.
- Lunch (*le déjeuner*) is served between 12 and 2 pm. The evening meal (*le dîner*) is normally served between 8 and 10 pm.
- In the restaurants you will be able to choose between the fixed-price menu with several courses (*le menu*) and the *à la carte* menu, where you may have as few or as many courses as you like.

● **Tipping:** if the menu or bill says '*Service compris*', you need not leave a tip. If you cannot see any indication, ask whether the tip is included (see page 46), or look to see if it has been added on to the bottom of the bill. The tip should be about 15% of the bill.

I'm hungry	J'ai faim *jay faŋ*
I'm thirsty	J'ai soif *jay swaf*
Can you recommend a good restaurant?	Pouvez-vous recommander un bon restaurant? *poovay voo rekomahŋday uŋ boŋ restorahŋ?*
Are there any inexpensive restaurants round here?	Y a-t-il des restaurants pas très chers près d'ici? *yateel day restorahŋ pah treh shehr preh deesee?*
I'd like to reserve a table for four	Je voudrais réserver une table pour quatre personnes *je voodreh rayservay ewn tabl poor katr pehrson*
for 8 o'clock	à 8 heures *a weet err*

Could we have a table . . .	Pourriez-vous nous mettre . . . *pooryay voo noo mehtr . . .*
. . . in the corner	. . . dans le coin *dahŋ le kwaŋ*
. . . by the window	. . . à côté de la fenêtre *a kohtay de la fenehtr*
. . . outside	. . . sur la terrace *sewr la terras*
. . . in a non-smoking area	. . . dans un endroit pour les non-fumeurs *dahŋzun ahŋdrwa poor lay noŋ fewmerr*

Ordering snacks

Give me ...	Donnez-moi ... *donay mwa ...*
I'd like ...	Je voudrais ... *je voodreh ...*
We'd like ...	Nous voudrions ... *noo voodreeoŋ ...*
... a beer	... une bière *ewn byehr*
... two white coffees	... deux crèmes *der krehm*
	... deux cafés au lait *der kafay oh leh*
... one black coffee	... un café nature *uŋ kafay natewr*
	... un café noir *uŋ kafay nwar*
... an espresso	... un café express *uŋ kafay esprehs*
... a fruit juice	... un jus de fruits *uŋ jew de frwee*
... a hamburger	... un hamburger *uŋ ahŋbewrgerr*
... a toasted cheese and ham sandwich	... un croque-monsieur *uŋ krok msyer*
... one/two pancakes	... une crêpe/deux crêpes *ewn krehp/der krehp*
... some chips (French fries)	... des frites *day freet*
What sort of sandwiches do you have?	Qu'est-ce que vous avez comme sandwiches? *kehske vooz avay kom saŋdveesh?*

I'll have a . . . sandwich	Je prends un sandwich au . . . *je prahŋ uŋ sahŋdveesh* *oh . . .*
. . . cheese	. . . fromage *fromaj*
. . . ham	. . . jambon *jahŋboŋ*
. . . pâté	. . . pâté *pahtay*
. . . sausage	. . . salami *salamee*

You may hear:

Vous avez choisi? *vooz avay shwazee?*	Have you chosen?
Et pour suivre? *ay poor sweevr?*	Anything to follow?
C'est tout? *seh too?*	Is that all?
Je vous recommande ceci *je voo rekomahŋd sesee*	I recommend this
Qu'est-ce que vous allez boire? *kehske vooz alay bwar?*	What would you like to drink?
Nous n'avons pas de . . . *noo navoŋ pah de . . .*	We don't have any . . .

You may see:

Menu à prix fixe	Set menu
Garniture au choix	Choice of accompanying vegetables
Supplément	Extra charge
Pour deux personnes	For two people

Ordering a meal

Is there a table available, please?	Y a-t-il une table de libre, s'il vous plaît? *yateel ewn tabl de leebr, seel voo pleh?*
There are two/three/four of us	Nous sommes deux/trois/quatre *noo som der/trwa/katr*
Will you bring me . . . ?	Voudriez-vous m'apporter . . . ? *voodreeay voo maportay*
. . . the set menu	. . . le menu à prix fixe *le menew a pree feex*
. . . the à la carte menu	. . . la carte *la kart*
We'll have the 30-franc menu/ today's special menu	On prend le menu à trente francs/ du jour *on prahŋ le menew a trahŋt fraŋ/ dew joor*

I'll have . . .	Je prends . . . *je prahŋ . . .*

. . . the cold meat	. . . la charcuterie *la sharkewtree*
. . . the salad	. . . la salade/les crudités *la salad/lay krewdeetay*
. . . the soup	. . . le potage/la soupe *le potaj/la soop*
. . . today's special	. . . le plat du jour *le pla dew joor*

Waiter!	Monsieur! *msyer!*
Waitress!	Mademoiselle! *mamzehl!*

Excuse me, I haven't got a . . .	Excusez-moi, je n'ai pas de . . . *ehxkewzay mwa, jnay pah de . . .*
. . . ashtray	. . . cendrier *sahŋdreeay*
. . . cup	. . . tasse *tas*
. . . fork	. . . fourchette *foorsheht*
. . . glass	. . . verre *vehr*
. . . knife	. . . couteau *kootoh*
. . . plate	. . . assiette *asyeht*
. . . saucer	. . . soucoupe *sookoop*
. . . spoon	. . . cuillère *kweeyehr*
cover charge	le couvert *le koovehr*
Do you have any vegetarian dishes?	Avez-vous des plats végétariens? *avay voo day pla vayjaytaryaŋ?*
that's enough	ça suffit *sa sewfee*
tipping not allowed	pourboire interdit *poorbwar aŋtehrdee*
Just a small portion	Juste une petite portion *jewst ewn pteet porsyoŋ*
Can I have more . . .	Un peu plus de . . . , s'il vous plaît *uŋ per plew de . . . seel voo pleh*

Describing food

It's ...	C'est ... *seh ...*
... delicious	... délicieux *dayleesyer*
... burnt	... brûlé *brewlay*
... just right	... à point *a pwaŋ*
... overcooked	... trop cuit *troh kwee*
... well done	... bien cuit *byaŋ kwee*
... too salty	... trop salé *troh salay*
... too sweet	... trop sucré *troh sewkray*

You may hear:

Suivez-moi, s'il vous plaît *sweevay mwa, seel voo pleh*	Follow me, please
Vouz avez choisi? *vooz avay shwazee?*	Have you chosen?
Que voulez-vous pour commencer? *ke voolay voo poor komaŋsay?*	What would you like to start?
Et pour suivre? *ay poor sweevr?*	And to follow?
Et comme boisson? *ay kom bwasoŋ?*	And what would you like to drink?
Bon appétit! *bonapaytee!*	Enjoy your meal!

39

Understanding the menu

Hors d'oeuvres   *Starters*

assiette anglaise
asyeht ahŋglehz
assorted cold roast meats

assiette de charcuterie
asyeht de sharkewtree
assorted cold (pork) meats

crudités
krewdeetay
salad of raw vegetables

hors d'oeuvre variés
or dervr vareeay
assorted hors d'oeuvres

jambon
jahŋbon
ham

oeufs
er
eggs

pâté
pahtay
pâté

salade mêlée
salad mehlay
mixed salad

saucisson
sohseesoŋ
sausage

Soupes   *Soups*

bouillon/consommé
booyoŋ/koŋsomay
clear soup

crème/velouté
krehm/vlootay
cream soups

potage
potaj
thick soup

pot-au-feu
pot oh fer
thick vegetable soup with meat

soupe du jour
soop dew joor
soup of the day

soupe à l'oignon
soop a lonyoŋ
French onion soup

● *Omelettes*   *Omelettes*

omelette nature   plain omelette
omleht natewr

omelette aux   mushroom omelette
champignons
omleht oh shahŋpeenyoŋ

omelette au jambon   ham omelette
omleht oh jahŋboŋ

● *Poissons*   *Fish dishes*

anchois   anchovies
ahŋshwa

cabillaud/morue   cod
kabeeyoh/morew

carrelet   plaice
karelay

crevettes   shrimps
kreveht

écrevisses   crayfish
aykrevees

harengs   herring
arahŋ

homard   lobster
omar

huîtres   oysters
weetr

langoustines/scampi   prawns/scampi
lahŋgoosteen/scahŋpee

moules   mussels
mool

saumon   salmon
sohmoŋ

thon   tuna
toŋ

truite   trout
trweet

● *Viande*

Meat and poultry dishes

agneau *anyoh*	lamb
bifteck *beeftehk*	steak
saignant *sehnyahŋ*	rare
à point *a pwaŋ*	medium
bien cuit *byaŋ kwee*	well done
boeuf *berf*	beef
charcuterie *sharkewtree*	pork products
côte *koht*	rib
côtelette *kohtleht*	chop
dinde *daŋd*	turkey
filet *feelay*	fillet
lapin *lapaŋ*	rabbit
lard *lar*	bacon
poulet *pooleh*	chicken
rosbif *rosbeef*	roast beef
porc *por*	pork

veau *voh*	veal
volailles *vola-y*	poultry

● *Légumes, riz et pâtes* — *Vegetables, rice and pasta*

asperges *aspehrj*	asparagus
betterave *behtrahv*	beetroot
carottes *karot*	carrots
champignons *shaŋpeenyoŋ*	mushrooms
choucroûte *shookroot*	sauerkraut
chou-fleur *shooflerr*	cauliflower
épinards *aypeenar*	spinach
haricots blancs *areekoh blahŋ*	haricot beans
haricots verts *areekoh vehr*	green beans
maïs *maees*	sweetcorn
nouilles *nooye*	noodles
pâtes *paht*	pasta
petits pois *ptee pwah*	peas
oignons *onyoŋ*	onions

pommes de terre *pom de tehr*	potatoes
duchesse/mousseline *dewshehs/moosleen*	mashed
nature/vapeur *natewr/vaperr*	boiled/steamed
pommes frites *pom freet*	chips (french fries)
riz *ree*	rice
salade *salad*	lettuce

● *Desserts*   *Desserts*

fraises à la crème *frehz ala krehm*	strawberries and cream
framboises à la crème *frahŋbwaz ala krehm*	raspberries and cream
glace à la vanille *glas ala vaneeye*	vanilla ice-cream
glace au citron *glas oh seetroŋ*	lemon ice-cream
pâtisseries *pahteesree*	cakes
pêche melba *pehsh mehlba*	peaches with ice-cream
tarte aux pommes *tart oh pom*	apple tart
aux cerises *oh sreez*	cherry tart
aux fraises *oh frehz*	strawberry tart
yaourt *yaoor*	yoghurt

● *Fruits et fromages*　　*Fruit and cheese*

ananas *anana*	pineapple
bananes *banan*	bananas
fraises *frehz*	strawberries
framboises *frahŋbwaz*	raspberries
fromage *fromaj*	cheese
oranges *orahŋj*	oranges
pamplemousse *pahŋplemoos*	grapefruit
poires *pwar*	pears
pommes *pom*	apples
prunes *prewn*	plums
abricots *abreekoh*	apricots
brugnons *brewnyoŋ*	nectarines
cassis *kasees*	blackcurrant
cerises *sereez*	cherries
citron *seetroŋ*	lemon
pêches *pehsh*	peaches
raisins *rehzaŋ*	grapes

Paying

Waiter! Will you bring the bill (check), please?	Monsieur! Voulez-vous apporter l'addition, s'il vous plaît? *msyer! voolay voo aportay ladeesyoŋ, seel voo pleh?*
Is service included?	Est-ce que le service est compris? *ehske le sehrvees eh koŋpree?*
Is the cover charge included?	Est-ce que le couvert est compris? *ehske le koovehr eh koŋpree?*
Do you accept traveller's cheques?	Est-ce que vous acceptez les chèques de voyage? *ehske vooz aksehptay lay shehk de vwayaj?*
Have you got change?	Avez-vous de la monnaie? *avay voo de la moneh?*
Keep the change	Gardez la monnaie *garday la moneh*
This is for you	Voici pour vous *vwasee poor voo*
Excuse me, there's a mistake	Excusez-moi, il y a erreur *ehxkewzay mwa, eelya ehrerr*

I/we had . . .	On a pris . . . *oŋ a pree . . .*
. . . the fixed-price meal	. . . le menu à prix fixe *le menew a pree feex*
. . . a bottle of . . .	. . . une bouteille de . . . *ewn booteh-y de . . .*
. . . the roast beef	. . . le rosbif *le rosbeef*

How much is that?	C'est combien, ça? *seh koŋbyaŋ, sa?*
But you have put . . . francs on the bill (check)	Mais vous avez mis . . . francs sur l'addition *meh vooz avay mee . . . frahŋ sewr ladeesyon*
I/we ordered . . .	On a commandé . . . *oŋ a komahŋday . . .*
I/we didn't order . . .	Mais on n'a pas commandé . . . *meh oŋ na pah komahŋday . . .*
You have put it on the bill (check)	Vous l'avez mis sur l'addition *voo lavay mee sewr ladeesyon*
You are wrong	Vous avez tort *vooz avay tor*
You are right	Vouz avez raison *vooz avay rehzoŋ*

You may hear:

Le service est compris *le sehrvees eh koŋpree*	Service is included
Le service n'est pas compris *le sehrvees neh pah koŋpree*	Service isn't included
Voulez-vous du café? *voolay voo dew kaffay?*	Would you like coffee?
Voulez-vous un dessert? *voolay voo uŋ daysehr?*	Would you like a dessert?
Il n'y en a pas *eel nyahŋ a pah*	We don't have any
Je vais le changer tout de suite *je veh le shahŋjay toot sweet*	I'll change it right away

47

Drinks

I'd like a . . . . of	J'aimerais . . . . de *jehmereh . . . . de*
. . . bottle	. . . une bouteille *ewn booteh-y*
. . . half bottle	. . . une demi-bouteille *ewn dmee booteh-y*
. . . carafe	. . . une carafe *ewn karaf*
. . . glass	. . . un verre *uŋ vehr*
red wine	vin rouge *vaŋ rooj*
white wine	vin blanc *vaŋ blahŋ*
rosé	rosé *rohzay*
dry	sec *sehk*
sweet	doux *doo*
sparkling	mousseux *moosser*
a (double) whisky	un whisky (double) *uŋ weeskee (doobl)*
a gin (and tonic)	un gin (-tonic) *uŋ djeen (-toneek)*
neat	sec *sehk*
on the rocks	avec des glaçons *avehk day glasoŋ*

● For other drinks, see page 110

ENTERTAINMENT AND SPORT

- There are many varieties of sport and entertainment to be found throughout the whole of France. For further details about those listed below, ask at your local travel agency, or the French Government Tourist Office in London (178 Piccadilly, tel 01 499 6911), the *Office de Tourisme* at 127 Champs Elysées, Paris (Métro George V), or at other *Offices de Tourisme* at the main-line railway stations in Paris and all French cities. In the smaller towns, the *Syndicat d'Initiative* (SI) and the local *auberge de jeunesse* (youth hostel) will have information. Elsewhere, look for the ⓘ sign.
- **Cycling:** ask at any French railway station for a list of stations from which cycles may be hired. The rates are not dear, and there are reductions for longer hire. Cycling is not pleasant on the major roads, but the minor roads can be delightful.
  A useful address is: Bicy-Club de France, 8, Place de la Porte-Champeret, 75017 Paris, tel (1) 766 55 92.

- **Horse riding:** travel by trekking (*randonnée à cheval*), caravan (*roulotte*) or carriage (*calèche*) are all possible.
- **Canal holidays:** there is a vast network of canals, providing beautiful and leisured holidays. The *Canal du Midi* and the *Canal de Bourgogne* have many locks to negotiate, but the scenery is your reward. For the most part, no charge is made for the locks, but you are expected to help.
- **Running:** two Parisian events are the *marathon de Paris* in Spring, and the Figaro cross-country race in November.
- *Son et lumière:* these spectacles take place at night in places of historical interest such as the Château of Versailles. Coloured lights play upon the buildings to give atmosphere, while taped voices with music give an account of past events there. Occasionally live actors are used.
- It is customary to tip the usherette in the cinema or theatre 1F per person.
- There are also festivals of music (classical music, opera or jazz), dance, theatre, cinema, folklore and science-fiction, and many religious celebrations throughout the year. You can buy magazines such as *Pariscope* in Paris and *Le Bulletin* in Brussels which list the current week's entertainments as well as restaurants, trips etc.
- The *Office de Tourisme* can tell you the exact dates each year for sporting events such as the Tour de France.
- Walking holidays (*randonnées*) are very popular in the mountainous regions of France, such as the Auvergne and the Massif Central. Details of routes can be obtained from the local *Syndicat d'Initiative*.
- Discos and nightclubs (*boîtes*) are to be found in most large towns. They do not generally get going until 11pm or midnight, but often stay open until dawn. Entrance fees can be expensive, as can drinks.
- One of the most popular ways of spending an evening is simply to sit on the terrace of a bar enjoying a drink with friends and watching the world go by.

At the cinema or theatre

What's on at the cinema (movies)?	Qu'est-ce qu'il y a au cinéma? *kehskeelya oh seenayma?*
What's on at the theatre?	Qu'est-ce qu'on joue au théâtre? *kehskoŋ joo oh tayahtr?*

Is it . . . ?	Est-ce que c'est . . . ? *ehske seh . . . ?*

. . . an American film	. . . un film américain *uŋ feelm amayreekaŋ*
. . . a cartoon	. . . un dessin animé *uŋ dehsaŋ aneemay*
. . . a comedy	. . . un film comique *uŋ feelm komeek*
. . . a detective film	. . . un film policier *uŋ feelm poleesyay*
. . . a documentary	. . . un documentaire *uŋ dokewmahŋtehr*
. . . a gangster film	. . . un film de gangsters *uŋ feelm de gahŋgstehr*
. . . a horror film	. . . un film d'épouvante *uŋ feelm daypoovahŋt*
. . . a romance	. . . un film d'amour *uŋ feelm damoor*
. . . a tragedy	. . . une tragédie *ewn trajaydee*
. . . a western	. . . un western *uŋ wehstehrn*
. . . suitable for children	. . . pour les enfants *poor layzahŋfahŋ*
. . . a new release	. . . une nouveauté *ewn noovohtay*

Is it . . . ?	Est-ce qu'il est . . . ? *ehskeel eh . . . ?*
. . . in black and white	. . . en noir et blanc *ahŋ nwar ay blahŋ*
. . . dubbed	. . . doublé *dooblay*
. . . in English	. . . en anglais *ahn ahŋgleh*
. . . in colour	. . . en couleurs *ahŋ koolerr*
. . . with the original sound track	. . . en version originale *ahŋ vehrsyoŋ oreejeenal*
Are there sub-titles?	Est-ce qu'il y a des sous-titres? *ehskeelya day soo teetr?*
Who's in it?	Qui joue? *kee joo?*
How much is a seat . . . ?	Combien coûte une place . . . ? *koŋbyaŋ koot ewn plas . . . ?*
. . . in the balcony	. . . au balcon *oh balkoŋ*
. . . in the stalls	. . . à l'orchestre *a lorkehstr*
	. . . au parterre *oh partehr*
. . . near the stage	. . . près de la scène *preh de la sehn*
. . . for an adult	. . . pour adulte *poor adewlt*
. . . for a child	. . . pour enfant *poor ahŋfahŋ*

Is there a special price . . . ?	Est-ce qu'il y a un tarif spécial . . . ? *ehskeelya uŋ tareef spaysyal . . . ?*
. . . for children	. . . pour les enfants *poor layz ahŋfahŋ*
. . . for a group	. . . pour un groupe *poor uŋ groop*
. . . for students	. . . pour les étudiants *poor layz aytewdyahŋ*
. . . for pensioners	. . . pour les retraités *poor lay retraytay*
. . . for the unemployed	. . . pour les chômeurs *poor lay shohmerr*

Booking

I'd like . . .	Je voudrais . . . *je voodreh . . .*
. . . two seats in the stalls	. . . deux orchestres *derz orkehstr*
. . . four seats together in the stalls	. . . quatre places ensemble au parterre *katr plas ahŋsahŋble oh partehr*
. . . a seat near the screen	. . . une place près de l'écran *ewn plas preh de laykrahŋ*
. . . a seat not too far back	. . . une place pas trop loin *ewn plas pah troh lwaŋ*
. . . a seat in the middle	. . . une place vers le milieu *ewn plas vehr le meelyer*
. . . a ticket for the afternoon performance	. . . un billet pour la matinée *uŋ beeyay poor la mateenay*

Times

At what time does . . . begin/end?	A quelle heure commence/finit . . . ? *a kehl err komahŋs/feenee . . . ?*
. . . the afternoon performance	. . . la matinée *la mateenay*
. . . the first performance	. . . la première séance *la premyehr sayahŋs*
. . . the last performance	. . . la dernière séance *la dehrnyehr sayahŋs*
. . . the interval	. . . l'entracte *lahŋtrakt*
. . . half-time	. . . la mi-temps *la mee tahŋ*
Has the performance begun?	Est-ce que la séance a commencé? *ehske la sayahŋs a komahŋsay?*
Can we order drinks in the interval?	Est-ce qu'on peut commander des boissons pour l'entracte? *ehskoŋ per komahŋday day bwassoŋ poor lahŋtrakt?*
Is there a matinée performance?	Est-ce qu'il y a une matinée? *ehskeelya ewn mateenay?*
Is there a cloakroom?	Est-ce qu'il y a un vestiaire? *ehskeelya uŋ vestyehr?*
Where can I buy a programme?	Où est-ce que je peux acheter un programme? *oo ehske je per ashtay uŋ program?*
Is there access for wheelchairs?	Est-ce que les fauteuils roulants peuvent y entrer? *ehske lay fohte-y roolahŋ perv ee ahŋtray?*

Opinions

What did you think of it?	Qu'est'ce que tu en as pensé? *kehske tew ahn a pahŋsay?*

It was . . .	Il était . . . *eel ayteh . . .*

. . . awful	. . . affreux *afrer*
. . . boring	. . . ennuyeux *ahnweeyer*
. . . fantastic	. . . chouette *shooeht*
. . . frightening	. . . effrayant *ehfrayahŋ*
. . . funny	. . . amusant *amewzahŋ*
. . . quite interesting	. . . assez intéressant *asay aŋtayrehsahŋ*
. . . very interesting	. . . très intéressant *trehz aŋtayrehsahŋ*

You may hear:	
il est défendu de fumer *eel eh dayfahndew de* *fewmay*	smoking not allowed
ce n'est pas permis *se neh pah pehrmee*	it is not allowed
votre billet, s'il vous plaît *votr beeay seel voo pleh*	your ticket, please
programmes! *program!*	programmes!

Other entertainments

Is/are there . . . near here?	Est-ce qu'il y a . . . près d'ici? *ehskeelya . . . preh deesee?*
. . . in the town	. . . en ville *ahŋ veel?*
. . . that you can recommend	. . . que vous pouvez recommander *ke voo poovay rekomahŋday*
. . . a boxing match	. . . un match de boxe *uŋ match de box*
. . . a circus	. . . un cirque *uŋ seerk*
. . . a concert	. . . un concert *uŋ koŋsehr*
. . . a disco	. . . une discothèque *ewn deeskotehk*
. . . a football (soccer) match	. . . un match de football *uŋ match de fewtbohl*
. . . a golf course	. . . un terrain de golf *un tehraŋ de golf*
. . . horse racing	. . . des courses de chevaux *day koors de shvoh*
. . . motor racing	. . . des courses d'auto *day koors dohtoh*
. . . a (musical) festival	. . . un festival *uŋ fehsteeval*
. . . a fun fair	. . . une fête foraine *ewn feht forehn*
. . . a son-et-lumière	. . . un son-et-lumière *uŋ soŋ ay lewmyehr*
. . . a sports complex	. . . un centre sportif *un sahŋtr sporteef*

. . . a swimming pool (indoor)	. . . une piscine couverte *ewn peeseen koovehrt*
. . . a swimming pool (outdoor)	. . . une piscine en plein air *ewn peeseen ahŋ plehnehr*
. . . a swimming pool (heated)	. . . une piscine chauffée *ewn peeseen shohfay*
. . . a skating rink	. . . une patinoire *ewn pateenwar*
. . . tennis courts	. . . des courts de tennis *day koor de tehnees*
. . . any walks	. . . des promenades *day promnad*
	. . . des randonnées *day rahŋdonay*

Do you like . . . ?	Aimez-vous . . . ? *ehmay voo . . . ?*
I like . . .	J'aime . . . *jehm . . .*

. . . boxing	. . . la boxe *la box*
. . . the cinema	. . . le cinéma *le seenayma*
. . . concerts	. . . les concerts *lay koŋsehr*
. . . cricket	. . . le cricket *le kreekeht*
. . . discos	. . . les discos *lay deeskoh*
. . . fishing	. . . la pêche *la pehsh*
. . . football	. . . le football *le fewtbohl*

. . . gymnastics	. . . la gymnastique *la jeemnasteek*
. . . skiing	. . . le ski *le skee*
. . . swimming	. . . la natation *la natasyoŋ*
. . . tennis	. . . le tennis *le taynees*
. . . walking	. . . les promenades *lay promnad*
. . . winter sports	. . . les sports d'hiver *lay spor deevehr*
. . . playing cards	. . . jouer aux cartes *jooay oh kart*
. . . playing computer games	. . . jouer aux jeux d'ordinateur *jooay oh jer dordeenaterr*

What does it cost to go in?	Quel est le prix d'entrée? *kehl eh le pree dahŋtray?*
What is the cost per hour/per day?	Quel est le tarif par heure/par jour? *kehl eh le tareef par err/par joor?*
Is there tuition available?	Peut-on prendre des cours? *pertoŋ prahŋdr day koor?*

Can I hire . . . ?	Est-ce que je peux louer . . . ? *ehske je per looay . . . ?*

. . . a bicycle	. . . un vélo *uŋ vayloh*
. . . a tennis racquet	. . . une raquette de tennis *ewn rakeht de taynees*
. . . all the equipment	. . . tout l'équipement *too laykeepmahŋ*
. . . skis	. . . des skis *day skee*

By the sea

Can I hire . . . ?	Est-ce que je peux louer . . . ? *ehske je per looay . . . ?*
. . . a deck chair	. . . une chaise longue *ewn shehz lohŋg*
. . . a motor boat	. . . un canot à moteur *uŋ kanoh a moterr*
. . . a rowing boat	. . . une barque à rames *ewn bark a ram*
. . . a windsurfer (sailboard)	. . . une planche à voile *ewn plahnsh a vwal*
. . . a surf board	. . . une planche de surf *ewn plahŋsh de sewrf*
. . . a swimsuit	. . . un maillot de bain *uŋ mayoh de baŋ*
. . . a towel	. . . une serviette *ewn sehrvyeht*
Is it safe to swim?	Est-ce qu'on peut nager sans danger? *ehskoŋ per najay sahn dahŋjay?*
Is there a lifeguard?	Y a-t-il un surveillant de plage? *yateel uŋ sewrveh-yahŋ de plaj?*
Does the beach have shingle or sand?	Est-ce que la plage est de galets ou de sable? *ehske la plaj eh de galeh oo de sabl?*
When is high/low tide?	C'est quand, la marée haute/basse? *seh kahŋ la maray oht/bas?*
Is it safe for children?	Est-ce sans danger pour les enfants? *ehs sahŋ dahŋjay poor layzahŋfahŋ?*

Skiing

skates	des patins *day pataŋ*
ski boots	des chaussures de ski *day shohsewr de skee*
ski equipment	un équipement de ski *uŋ aykeepmahŋ de skee*
skis	des skis *day skee*
a sledge	une luge *ewn lewj*
to ski	faire du ski *fehr dew skee*
skiing lessons	des leçons de ski *day lesoŋ de skee*
ski lift	un téléski *uŋ taylayskee*
ski run	une piste *ewn peest*
bindings	des fixations *day feeksasyoŋ*
ski pants	un fuseau *uŋ fewzoh*
ski sticks	des bâtons de ski *day bahtoŋ de skee*
lift pass	un forfait *uŋ forfeh*
ski instructor	un moniteur/une monitrice *uŋ moneeterr/ewn moneetrees*
ski jumping	le saut à skis *le soht a skee*
ski resort	une station de ski *ewn stasyoŋ de skee*
ski slopes	des pentes de ski *day pahŋt de skee*

Visiting a town

Where is . . . ?	Où se trouve . . . ? *oo se troov . . . ?*
. . . the tourist information office	. . . le Syndicat d'Initiative *le saŋdeeka deeneesyateev*
. . . the castle	. . . le château *le shahtoh*
. . . the cathedral	. . . la cathédrale *la kataydral*
. . . the market	. . . le marché *le marshay*
. . . the museum	. . . le musée *le mewzay*
. . . the palace	. . . le palais *le paleh*
. . . the shopping centre	. . . le centre commercial *le sahŋtr komehrsyal*
Is it open on Sundays?	C'est ouvert le dimanche? *seht oovehr le deemahŋsh?*
Can I take photos?	Il est permis de prendre des photos? *eel eh perhrmee de prahŋdr day fotoh?*
Do you have a guidebook in English?	Avez-vous un guide en anglais? *avay voo uŋ geed ahn ahŋgleh?*
Is there a guided tour?	Y a-t-il une visite guidée? *yateel ewn veezeet geeday?*
Do you have any postcards?	Avez-vous des cartes postales? *avay voo day kart postal?*

Meeting people

What's your name?	Comment vous appelez-vous? *komahŋ vooz aplay voo?*
My name is . . .	Je m'appelle . . . *je mapehl . . .*
Pleased to meet you	Enchanté(e) *ahŋshahŋtay*
Is this seat free?	Es-ce que cette place est libre? *ehske seht plas eh leebr?*
Do you mind if I smoke?	Est-ce que cela vous dérange si je fume? *ehske sla voo dayrahŋj see je fewm?*
Do you have a light?	Vous avez du feu? *vooz avay dew fer?*
Would you like to . . . . ?	Voulez-vous . . . ? *voolay voo . . . ?*
. . . dance	. . . danser *dahŋsay*
. . . have something to eat/ drink	. . . manger/boire quelque chose *mahŋjay/bwar kehlke shohz*
I'm with my . . .	Je suis avec . . . *je swee avehk . . .*
. . . family	. . . ma famille *ma famee-y*
. . . friends	. . . mes ami(e)s *mayz amee*
. . . boyfriend	. . . mon copain *mon kopaŋ*
. . . girlfriend	. . . ma copine *ma kopeen*

. . . husband	. . . mon mari *mon maree*
. . . wife	. . . ma femme *ma fam*

Where are you from?	D'où venez-vous? *doo venay voo?*
I'm from . . .	Je suis de . . . *jswee de . . .*
I'm on holiday	Je suis en vacances *jswee ahŋ vakahŋs*
I'm studying here	Je fais des études ici *je feh dayz aytewd eesee*
I'm here on business	Je suis en voyage d'affaires *jsweez ahŋ vwayaj daffehr*
What do you do?	Quelle est votre profession? *kehl eh votr profehsyoŋ?*
What are you studying?	Qu'étudiez-vous? *kaytewdyay voo?*

Reactions

It's . . .	C'est . . . *seh . . .*
. . . wonderful/great	. . . chouette *shweht*
. . . (very) beautiful	. . . (très) beau *treh boh*
. . . interesting	. . . intéressant *aŋtayrehsahŋ*
. . . horrible	. . . horrible *oreeble*
. . . boring	. . . ennuyeux *ahnwee-er*

Business expressions

I'm ...	Je suis ... *jswee ...*
... Mr Smith	... M Smith *msyer smeeth*
... Mrs Smith	... Mme Smith *madam smeeth*
... Miss Smith	... Mlle Smith *mamzel smeeth*
I'm from ... (company)	Je représente la compagnie ... *je reprayzahnt la koŋpanyee ...*
I have an appointment with ...	J'ai un rendez-vous avec ... *jay uŋ rahŋday voo avehk ...*
Could I speak to ...	Est-ce que je peux parler avec ... *ehske je per parlay avehk ...*
... the sales manager	... le directeur commercial *le deerehkterr komehrsyahl*
... the personnel manager	... le chef du personnel *le shehf dew pehrsonehl*
Here is my card	Voici ma carte *vwasee ma kart*
I'm sorry I'm late	Je suis désolé(e), je suis en retard *jswee dayzolay, jswee ahŋ retar*
I'm in the hotel ...	Je suis à l'hôtel ... *jswee a lohtehl ...*
Please ask him/her to call me	Voulez-vous lui demander de m'appeler? *voolay voo lwee demahŋday de maplay?*

HEALTH

- It is well worth your while to ask at your local DHSS for form CM-1, about a month or more before your holiday. This must be filled in and returned to the DHSS *before* you go on your holiday. You will be given Form E111 to take on holiday with you. A single form will cover a whole family.
- If you then have to pay a French doctor or hospital, get a receipt (*une quittance*) and present it to the French Sickness Insurance Office with your form E111. You will be given back up to 80% of the charges.
- In order to claim money back on prescriptions, stick the price labels from the medicines on the prescription sheet.
- You can top up your free health insurance with temporary health insurance from a broker's or travel agent. This usually costs very little for a short holiday.

At the doctor's

My . . . hurts	J'ai mal . . . *jay mal . . .*
. . . arm	. . . au bras *oh bra*
. . . back	. . . au dos *oh doh*
. . . chest	. . . à la poitrine *a la pwatreen*
. . . eyes	. . . aux yeux *oh zyer*
. . . head	. . . à la tête *a la teht*
. . . leg	. . . à la jambe *a la jahŋb*
. . . stomach	. . . à l'estomac *a lehstoma*
	. . . au ventre *oh vahntr*
. . . tooth	. . . aux dents *oh dahŋ*

I have asthma	J'ai de l'asthme *jay de lasme*
I am airsick	J'ai le mal de l'air *jay le mal de lehr*
I am carsick	J'ai le mal de la route *jay le mal de la root*
I am seasick	J'ai le mal de mer *jay le mal de mehr*
I have a cold	J'ai un rhume *jay uŋ rewm*
I am constipated	Je suis constipé *je swee koŋsteepay*

I am diabetic	Je suis diabétique *je swee deeabayteek*
I have diarrhoea	J'ai la diarrhée *jay la deearay*
	la colique *la koleek*
I have flu	J'ai la grippe *jay la greep*
I am allergic to antibiotics/ penicillin	J'ai une allergie aux antibiotiques/à la pénicilline *jay ewn alehrjee ohz ahŋteebeeoteek/a la payneeseeleen*
I have twisted my ankle	Je me suis tordu la cheville *je me swee tordew la sheveeye*
I have dizzy spells	J'ai des vertiges *jay day vehrteej*
I am epileptic	Je suis épileptique *je sweez aypeelehpteek*
I have a heart problem	J'ai des troubles cardiaques *jay day trooble kardeeak*
I have high blood pressure	Ma tension est trop élevée *ma tahŋsyoŋ eh trohp aylevay*
I feel shivery	J'ai des frissons *jay day freesoŋ*
I have been stung by a bee/ wasp	J'ai été piqué(e) par une abeille/une guêpe *jay aytay peekay par ewn abeh-y/ewn gehp*
I have period pains	J'ai les règles douloureuses *jay lay rehgl dooloorerz*
I feel sick	J'ai mal au coeur *jay mal oh kerr*
I have a sore throat	J'ai mal à la gorge *jay mal a la gorj*

I have a temperature	J'ai de la température *jay de la tahŋpayratewr*
	de la fièvre *de la fyehvr*
I have sunstroke	J'ai un coup de soleil *jay uŋ koo de soleh-y*
	une insolation *ewn aŋsolasyoŋ*
May I have a receipt?	Voulez-vous me donner une quittance? *voolay voo me donay ewn keetahŋs?*

You may hear:

Je vais vous donner . . . *je veh voo donay . . .*	I'm going to give you . . .
. . . une piqûre *ewn peekewr*	. . . an injection
. . . cette crème *seht krehm*	. . . this cream
. . . ce médicament *se maydeekamahŋ*	. . . this medicine
. . . ce sirop *se seeroh*	. . . this mixture
. . . une ordonnance *ewn ordonahŋs*	. . . a prescription
. . . ces pilules/ces cachets *say peelewl/say kashay*	. . . these pills
Allez au lit tout de suite *alay oh lee toot sweet*	Go to bed straight away
Gardez le lit pendant . . . jours *garday le lee pahŋdahŋ . . . joor*	Stay in bed for . . . days

Allez chez le dentiste *alay shay le dahŋteest*	Go to the dentists
Allez chez l'opticien *alay shay lopteesyaŋ*	Go to the optician
Qu'est-ce qu'il y a? *kehskeelya?*	What's the matter?
Où est-ce que vous avez mal? *oo ehske vooz avay mal?*	Where does it hurt?
Il faut prendre un médicament *eel foh prahŋdr uŋ maydeekamahŋ*	You must take some medicine

I've been in pain . . .	**J'ai mal depuis . . .** *jay mal depwee . . .*
. . . for a week	**. . . une semaine** *ewn smehn*
. . . for several days	**. . . plusieurs jours** *plewzyerr joor*
. . . since yesterday	**. . . hier** *yehr*
. . . since this morning	**. . . ce matin** *se mataŋ*
. . . for a few hours	**. . . quelques heures** *kehlkez err*

I had the same problem . . .	**J'ai eu le même problème . . .** *jay ew le mehm problehm . . .*
. . . last year	**. . . l'année dernière** *lanay dernyehr*
. . . a few years ago	**. . . il y a quelques années** *eelya kehlkezanay*
. . . two months ago	**. . . il y a deux mois** *eelya der mwa*

At the dentist's

Is that the dentist's waiting room?	C'est bien la salle d'attente du dentiste? *seh byan la sal datahnt dew dahnteest?*
Can I have an appointment with . . . please?	Est-ce que je peux prendre rendez-vous avec . . . s'il vous plaît? *ehske je per prahndr rahnday voo avehk . . . seel voo pleh?*
When is his surgery?	A quelle heure consulte-t-il? *a kehl err konsewlt teel?*
I have an awful toothache	J'ai très mal aux dents *jay treh mal oh dahn*
I'm insured	Je suis assuré(e) *je sweez asewray*

You may hear:

Qu'est-ce qu'il y a? *kehskeelya?*	What's the matter?
Il consulte cet après-midi *eel konsewlt seht apreh meedee*	There is a surgery this afternoon
Est-ce que vous avez mal? *ehske vooz avay mal?*	Are you in pain?
Est-ce que vous pouvez venir dans une heure? *ehske voo poovay veneer dahnz ewn err?*	Can you come in an hour?
Quel est votre nom? *kehl eh votr non?*	What's your name?
Vous êtes assuré(e)? *vooz eht asewray?*	Are you insured?
Quel dent vous fait mal? *kehl dahn voo feh mal?*	Which tooth hurts?

At the chemist's

May I have ...	Est-ce que je peux avoir ... *ehske je per avwar ...*
... an (antiseptic) cream	... une crème (antiseptique) *ewn krehm* *ahŋteesehpteek*
... some aspirin	... de l'aspirine *de laspeereen*
... a bandage	... un pansement *uŋ pahŋsmahŋ*
... some cream	... de la crème *de la krehm*
... a lotion	... une lotion *ewn lohsyoŋ*
... some medicine	... un médicament *uŋ maydeekamahŋ*
... a mixture	... un sirop *uŋ seeroh*
... a prescription	... une ordonnance *ewn ordonahŋs*
... these pills	... ces pilules *say peelewl*
	... ces cachets *say kashay*
... some sticking-plaster	... du sparadrap *dew sparadra*

Could you make up this prescription?	Voulez-vous préparer cette ordonnance? *voolay voo prayparay seht ordonahŋs?*
Do you have anything for ... ?	Avez-vous quelque chose contre ... ? *avay voo kehlke shohz koŋtr ... ?*

71

At the optician's

I've broken my glasses

J'ai cassé mes lunettes
jay kassay may lewneht

Can you repair them?

Pouvez-vous les réparer?
poovay voo lay rayparay?

When will they be ready?

Quand seront-elles prêtes?
kahŋ seroŋtehl preht?

Can you change the lenses?

Pouvez-vous changer les
verres?
*poovay voo shahŋjay lay
vehr?*

I'd like a case for my glasses

Je voudrais un étui à lunettes
*je voodreh uŋ aytwee a
lewneht*

I've lost one of my contact
lenses

J'ai perdu un verre de contact
*jay pehrdew uŋ vehr de
koŋtakt*

Have you any contact lense
liquid?

Avez-vous un produit pour
nettoyer les verres de contact?
*avay voo un prodwee poor
nehtwayay lay vehr de
koŋtakt?*

I have hard/soft lenses

J'ai des verres de contact
durs/souples
*jay day vehr de koŋtakt dewr/
soopl*

I'm short-sighted/long-
sighted

Je suis myope/presbyte
jswee myop/prehsbeet

I need some sunglasses

Il me faut des lunettes de
soleil
*eel me foh day lewneht de
soleh-y*

You may hear:

Portez-vous des verres de
contact durs ou souples?
*portay voo day vehr de
koŋtakt dewr oo soopl?*

Do you wear hard or soft
contact lenses?

- Write to *L'Office de Tourisme* in the city you plan to visit, or to the *Syndicat d'Initiative* (information bureau) in smaller towns. These will give you plenty of brochures and information about specialised holidays, local tours operators, travel agents, etc. Get the address from a good holiday guide, or try a letter using the name of the city for your address. An international reply coupon would be appreciated.

Travel by car

- See **Essential Information** for information about licences, car rental and other road information.
- The AA and RAC are a mine of information about travelling abroad. Or phone Paris (1) 544 39 93 (Direction de Routes, Ministère des Transports, 244 bd Saint-Germain, 75007 Paris).

- **Roads**: the *autoroutes* (motorways) are shown by the letter A on blue and white road signs.
  The *routes nationales* (main roads) have the prefix N or RN on the road signs.
  Ask at the AA or RAC, or write to any French Government Tourist Office for the English-language version of the *Bison-Futé* brochure, if you wish to know about minor, but less crowded routes through France. These have green and white road signs.
- Hitch-hiking (*l'autostop*) has more official recognition in France than in Britain. There are several organisations where drivers and hitchhikers can register, and suitable link-ups are arranged. The hitchhiker pays a fee, and can expect to pay some petrol costs. One such group is *Allostop*, 84 passage Brady, 75010 Paris (tel (1) 246 00 66), with several regional branches. A booklet *Le Manuel du Routard*, obtainable at newsagents', is a worthwhile buy if you can read French. However, with all hitch-hiking, caution is advised, especially for women.

Car rental

Where is the car rental agency?	Où se trouve l'agence de location de voitures? *oo se troov lajahŋs de lokasyoŋ de vwatewr?*
I'd like to hire a car	Je voudrais louer une voiture *je voodreh looay ewn vwatewr*
for one/two/three people	pour une/deux/trois personne(s) *poor ewn/der/trwa pehrson*
for a day/a week	pour un jour/une semaine *poor un joor/ewn smehn*
What are your charges per day/per kilometre?	Quels sont vos tarifs par jour/par kilomètre? *kel soŋ voh tareef par joor/par keelomehtr?*

How much is the insurance/ deposit?	Combien coûte l'assurance/la caution? *koŋbyaŋ koot lasewrahŋs/la kohsyoŋ?*
Will you write it down, please?	Voulez-vous l'écrire, s'il vous plaît? *voolay voo laykreer, seel voo pleh?*
What is the total cost?	Quel est le montant? *kehl eh le moŋtahŋ?*
Is it air-conditioned?	Est-ce qu'elle est climatisée? *ehskehl eh kleemateezay?*
Is there a radio?	Est-ce qu'il y a une radio? *ehskeelya ewn radyoh?*

Taking a taxi

Where can I find a taxi?	Où est-ce que je peux trouver un taxi? *oo ehske je per troovay uŋ taxee?*
I want to go to ...	Je veux aller à ... *je ver alay a ...*
... the airport	... l'aéroport *la-ayropor*
... the Hotel ...	... l'hôtel ... *lohtehl*
... the station	... la gare *la gar*
How much is it?	C'est combien? *seh koŋbyaŋ?*
It's near here	C'est près d'ici *seh preh deesee*

Will you . . . ?	Voulez-vous . . . ? *voolay voo . . . ?*
. . . carry my bags	. . . porter mes bagages *portay may bagaj*
. . . slow down	. . . ralentir *ralahŋteer*
. . . stop here	. . . vous arrêter ici *vooz arehtay eesee*
. . . wait for me	. . . m'attendre *matahŋdr*

At a garage or petrol station

Buying petrol

- *Essence* or *essence normale* is 2-star petrol
- *Essence super* is 4-star petrol
- Unleaded petrol is *sans plomb*
- You may find country garages shut between 12 and 2 pm
- Credit cards are not always accepted in payment for petrol, so make sure you have sufficient currency with you.

Where's the nearest petrol station?	Où se trouve la station-service la plus proche? *oo se troov la stasyoŋ sehrvees la plew prosh?*
Do you accept credit cards?	Est-ce que vous acceptez les cartes de crédit? *ehske vooz aksehptay lay kart de kraydee?*
Fill the tank, please	Faites le plein, s'il vous plaît *feht le plaŋ, seel voo pleh*
Give me . . . litres of 2 star/4 star (regular/premium)	Donnez-moi . . . litres d'ordinaire/de super *donay mwa . . . leetr dordeenehr/de sewpehr*

Give me . . . francs worth of 2 star/4 star, please	Donnez-moi de l'ordinaire/du super pour . . . francs, s'il vous plaît *donay mwa de lordeenehr/ dew sewpehr poor . . . frahŋ seel voo pleh*
How much is it a litre?	C'est combien le litre? *seh koŋbyaŋ le leetr?*
I'll have the 4 star/unleaded, please	Je prends le super/sans plomb s'il vous plaît *je prahŋ le sewpehr/sahŋ ploŋ seel voo pleh*
Will you check the oil too?	Voulez-vous vérifier l'huile aussi? *voolay voo vayreefyay lweel ohsee?*
Have you a road map?	Avez-vous une carte routière? *avay voo ewn kart rootyehr?*
How much do I owe you?	Je vous dois combien? *je voo dwa koŋbyaŋ?*
How far is it to the motorway?	L'autoroute est à quelle distance? *lohtohroot eht a kehl deestahŋs?*
How far is the nearest town?	La ville la plus proche est à quelle distance? *la veel la plew prosh ehta kehl deestahŋs?*
May we use the toilets?	Est-ce qu'on peut se servir des toilettes? *ehskoŋ per se sehrveer day twaleht?*
Do you have air for the tyres?	Avez-vous de l'air pour les pneus? *avay voo de lehr poor lay pner?*
Is there any water?	Y a-t-il de l'eau? *yateel de loh?*
I'd like a litre of oil	Je voudrais un litre d'huile *je voodreh uŋ leetr dweel*

Will you check . . .	Voulez-vous vérifier . . . *voolay voo vayreefyay . . .*
. . . the brakes	. . . les freins *lay fraŋ*
. . . the oil	. . . l'huile *lweel*
. . . the tyres	. . . les pneus *lay pner*
. . . the spare wheel	. . . la roue de secours *la roo de skoor*
. . . the water	. . . l'eau *loh*
. . . the tyre pressure	. . . la pression des pneus *la prehsyoŋ day pner*

attendant	le/la pompiste *le/la poŋpeest*
cash desk	la caisse *la kehs*
to check	vérifier *vayreefyay*
to clean	nettoyer *nehtwayay*
to inflate	gonfler *goŋflay*
petrol (gas)	l'essence *lehsahŋs*
2-star (regular)	ordinaire *ordeenehr*
4-star (premium)	super *sewpehr*
road map	la carte routière *la kart rootyehr*

You may hear:

Allez tout droit *alay too drwa*	Go straight on
C'est à cent mètres *sehta sahŋ mehtr*	It's 100 metres away
C'est loin *seh lwaŋ*	It's a long way
C'est là-bas *seh la bah*	It's over there
Super ou ordinaire? *sewpehr oo ordeenehr?*	Do you want 4 or 2 star (premium or regular)?
Le super est à . . . le litre *le sewpehr ehta . . . le leetr*	4-star (premium) . . . francs a litre
C'est tout? *seh too?*	Is that all?
Il faut aller à la caisse *eel foh alay a la kehs*	You'll have to go to the cash-desk
Nous n'en avons pas pour cette marque *noo nahŋ avoŋ pah poor seht mark*	We haven't got any for that make
Vous avez la clef, s'il vous plaît? *vooz avay la klay seel voo pleh?*	May I have the key, please?

Repairs

- In case of need, if your car is one of the following makes, you can phone to ask where the nearest service station is:
  Citroen (16) 05 24 24; Renault (1) 252 82 82; Peugeot-Talbot (1) 281 91 91.

What's the matter?	Qu'est-ce qu'il y a? *kehskeelya?*

My car is a Citroen/Renault/Peugeot	Ma voiture est une Citroen/Renault/Peugeot *ma vwatewr ehtewn seetrerŋ/renoh/perjoh*
My car's broken down	Je suis tombé(e) en panne *je swee toŋbay ahŋ pan*
Where is the nearest service station for Citroens/Renaults/Peugeots?	Où est la station-service la plus proche pour les Citroens/Renaults/Peugeots? *oo eh la stasyoŋ sehrvees la plew prosh poor lay seetrerŋ/renoh/perjoh?*
The car is near Nancy/Nice/Nantes	La voiture est près de Nancy/Nice/Nantes *La vwatewr eh preh de nahŋsee/nees/nahŋt*
I've run out of petrol (gas)	J'ai eu une panne d'essence *jay ew ewn pan dehsahŋs*
I've got a puncture (flat)	J'ai eu un pneu crevé *jay ew uŋ pner krevay*

I was rammed by . . .	J'ai été embouti(e) par . . . *jay aytay ahŋbootee par . . .*
I bumped into . . .	J'ai embouti . . . *jay ahŋbootee . . .*

. . . the car	. . . la voiture *la vwatewr*
. . . the lorry	. . . le camion *le kamyoŋ*
. . . the motor-bike	. . . la moto *la motoh*
. . . the bicycle	. . . la bicyclette *la beeseekleht*
. . . the pedestrian	. . . le piéton *le pyaytoŋ*

Can you repair the . . .	Pouvez-vous réparer . . .
	poovay voo rayparay . . .
The . . . isn't working	. . . ne marche pas
	ne marsh pah

. . . battery	. . . la batterie
	la batree
. . . brakes	. . . les freins
	lay fraŋ
. . . door	. . . la portière
	la portyehr
. . . exhaust	. . . l'échappement
	layshapmahŋ
. . . fan belt	. . . la courroie de ventilateur
	la koorwa de
	vahŋteelaterr
. . . headlights	. . . les phares
	lay far
. . . indicator	. . . le clignotant
	le kleenyotahŋ
. . . radiator	. . . le radiateur
	le radyaterr
. . . seat bealt	. . . la ceinture de sécurité
	la saŋtewr de
	saykewreetay
. . . spare wheel	. . . la roue de secours
	la roo de skoor
. . . steering wheel	. . . le volant
	le volahŋ
. . . window	. . . la glace
	la glas
. . . windscreen (windshield)	. . . le pare-brise
	le par breez
. . . windscreen wiper	. . . l'essuie-glace
	lehswee glas

A road accident

Look out!	Attention! *atahŋsyoŋ!*
Help!	Au secours! *oh skoor!*
Fire!	Au feu! *oh fer!*
Thieves!	Aux voleurs! *oh volerr!*
Will you call the police?	Voulez-vous appeler la police? *voolay vooz aplay la polees?*
I'll call an ambulance	Je vais appeler une ambulance *je vehz aplay ewn ahŋbewlahŋs*
Where can I find a phone booth?	Où est-ce que je peux trouver une cabine téléphonique? *oo ehske je per troovay ewn kabeen taylayfoneek?*
Are you better?	Est-ce que vous allez mieux? *ehske vooz alay myer?*
Is somebody going to make a report?	Est-ce qu'on va faire un constat? *ehskoŋ va fehr uŋ koŋsta?*
I'll give you my name and address	Je vais vous donner mon nom et mon addresse *je veh voo donay moŋ noŋ ay mon adrehs*
I had priority	C'est moi qui avait le droit *seh mwa kee aveh le drwa*
Is anybody injured?	Y a-t-il des blessés? *yateel day blessay?*

You may hear:

Vous avez attrapé une contravention *vooz avay atrapay ewn koŋtravahŋsyoŋ*	You have got a fine
Vous avez excédé la limitation de vitesse *vooz avay ehksayday la leemeetasyoŋ de veetehs*	You have exceeded the speed limit
Quel est votre numéro d'immatriculation? *kehl eh votre newmayroh deematreekewlasyoŋ?*	What is your registration number?
voiture immatriculée XFV 425 G *vwatewr eematreekewlay eex ehf vay katre sahŋ vaŋ saŋk jay*	car with registration no. XFV 425 G
Où est votre . . . ? *oo eh votr . . . ?*	*Where is your . . . ?*
. . . permis de conduire *pehrmee de koŋdweer*	. . . driving licence
. . . carte d'immatriculation *kart deematreekewlasyoŋ*	. . . registration certificate
. . . carte verte *kart vehrt*	. . . Green Card
. . . carte d'assurance *kart dassewrahŋs*	. . . certificate of insurance
. . . plaque de nationalité *plak de nasyonaleetay*	. . . nationality plate
Vous avez une pièce d'identité? *vooz avay ewn pyehs deedahŋteetay?*	Have you some identification?
Est-ce que les feux étaient rouges? *ehske lay fer ayteh rooj?*	Were the lights red?

Useful vocabulary

(snow) chains	les chaînes *lay shehn*
a fine	une contravention *ewn kontravahŋsyoŋ*
	une amende *ewn amahŋd*
passengers	les passagers *lay pasajay*
at the back	à l'arrière *a laryehr*
traffic lights	les feux *lay fer*
dipped headlights	les feux de croisement *lay fer de krwazmahŋ*
green light	le feu vert *le fer vehr*
red light	le feu rouge *le fer rooj*
rear lights	les feux arrière *lay ferz aryehr*
side lights	les feux de position *lay fer de pozeesyoŋ*
warning light	le voyant *le vwayahŋ*
warning sign	le panneau avertisseur *le panoh avehrteeserr*
to brake	freiner *frehnay*
to cross	traverser *travehrsay*
to collide with	entrer en collision avec *ahŋtray ahŋ koleezyoŋ avehk*
to have priority	avoir le droit *avwar le drwa*

to switch on (lights)	allumer *alewmay*
to switch off (lights)	éteindre *aytahŋdre*
to hurt	blesser *blehsay*
to knock down	renverser/écraser *rahnvehrsay/aykrazay*
to overtake	dépasser *daypasay*
to stop	s'arrêter *sarehtay*
I was careful	J'ai fait attention *jay feht atahŋsyoŋ*
I was careless	Je n'ai pas fait attention *jnay pah feht atahŋsyoŋ*
He was careless	Il n'a pas fait attention *eel na pah feht atahŋsyoŋ*
I've phoned	J'ai téléphoné *jay taylayfonay*
I'm cold	J'ai froid *jay frwa*
I'm hungry	J'ai faim *jay faŋ*
I'm thirsty	J'ai soif *jay swaf*
Are you hurt?	Etes-vous blessé(e)? *eht voo blehsay?*
Be careful!	Attention! *atahŋsyoŋ!*
I didn't know that . . .	Je ne savais pas que . . . *je ne saveh pah ke . . .*
you must	il faut *eel foh*
you must not	il ne faut pas *eel ne foh pah*

Travel by train

- Write to French Railways Ltd., 179 Piccadilly, London W1V 0BA (tel 01 409 1224) for information, timetables and brochures.
- Write to French Travel Service, Francis House, Francis Street, London SW1P 1DE (tel 01 828 8131) for information about special holiday packages using rail travel.
- French trains are modern, speedy and comfortable, with connecting bus and coach services to all parts of France.

  The **TGV** (high-speed train) runs from Paris to south-east France.

  Motorail services are available from Amiens, Boulogne, Calais, Dieppe, and Lille.

  Loisirail provides entertainment on certain trains to Béziers, Bordeaux, Clermont-Ferrand, Geneva, Marseilles, Paris, etc.

- There are many reductions available for children, young people and senior citizens, and off-peak travel (marked in blue on the SNCF timetables). Most main-line trains add a supplement to their fares for peak-time travel – marked in red on the SNCF timetables.

  There are also holiday-return tickets, party tickets, a Eurail pass, a France-Vacances card with bonus offers, etc.

  It is possible to buy your ticket on the train from the ticket collector (*contrôleur*), but you will be charged at the full rate plus a small fee.

- It is possible to book couchettes and sleeping cars on the spot at most stations when you have bought your rail ticket, but in high season advance booking is probably necessary.
- You must punch (*composter*) your own ticket in the date-stamping machine at the platform entrance. Otherwise you will have to pay an extra fee. You need not punch your ticket if it was bought outside France.

Is there a special price . . . ?	Est-ce qu'il y a un tarif spécial . . . ? *ehskeelya uŋ tareef spaysyal . . . ?*
. . . today	. . . aujourd'hui *ohjoordwee*
. . . for children	. . . pour les enfants *poor layz ahŋfahŋ*
. . . for students	. . . pour les étudiants *poor layz aytewdyahŋ*
. . . for senior citizens	. . . pour les personnes âgées *poor lay pehrsonzahjay*

A ticket for . . . please	Un billet pour . . . s'il vous plaît *uŋ beeyay poor . . . seel voo pleh*
A single (one-way)	un aller *uŋ alay*
A return (roundtrip)	un aller-retour *uŋ alay retoor*
first class	première classe *premyehr klas*
second class	seconde classe *zegoŋd klas*
How much is that?	C'est combien? *seh koŋbyaŋ?*
What time does the train leave?	Le train part à quelle heure? *le traŋ par a kehl err?*
Do I have to change?	Est-ce qu'il faut changer? *ehskeel foh shahŋjay?*
How long does it take?	Il faut mettre combien de temps pour arriver? *eel foh mehtr koŋbyaŋ de tahŋ poor areevay?*

Is this the right train for . . . ?	C'est bien le train pour . . . ? *seh byaŋ le traŋ poor . . . ?*
Is this seat free?	Est-ce que cette place est libre? *ehske seht plas eh leebr?*
I'm sorry/excuse me	Pardon *pardohŋ*

Which . . . is it to go to Calais?	Pour aller à Calais c'est quel(le) . . . ? *poor allay a kaleh seh kehl . . . ?*

. . . bus	. . . autobus *bews*
. . . bus stop	. . . arrêt *areh*
. . . connection	. . . correspondance *korehspoŋdahŋs*
. . . counter	. . . guichet *geeshay*
. . . coach	. . . car *kar*
. . . flight	. . . vol *vol*
. . . office	. . . bureau *bewroh*
. . . platform	. . . quai *keh*
. . . seat	. . . place *plas*
. . . station	. . . gare *gar*
. . . track/platform	. . . voie *vwa*

. . . train	. . . train *traŋ*
. . . exit	. . . sortie *sortee*
. . . entrance	. . . entrée *ahŋtray*

Which platform does the train leave from	Le train part de quelle voie? *le traŋ par de kehl vwa?*
At what time does the train for . . . leave?	A quelle heure part le train pour . . . ? *a kehl err par le traŋ poor . . . ?*

You may hear:	
Un aller simple ou un aller-retour? *uŋ alay sahŋpl oo uŋ alay retoor?*	Single or return (one-way or round trip)?
Première classe ou seconde classe? *premyehr klas oo zegoŋd klas?*	1st class or 2nd class?
Non, c'est un train direct *noŋ seht uŋ traŋ deerehkt*	No, it's a through train
De la voie numéro dix *de la vwa newmayroh dees*	From platform 10
Tous les vingt minutes *too lay vahŋ meenewt*	Every 20 minutes
occupé *okewpay*	taken
Votre billet, s'il vous plaît *votr beeyay seel voo pleh*	Could I see your ticket, please?
Il faut changer à . . . *eel foh shahŋjay a . . .*	You have to change at . . .

Travel by bus or coach

- The coach and bus services complement the railway network to reach into every corner of France, and are economical. Detailed timetables are obtainable from the SNCF (French Railways) stations and offices. They also publish a guide giving fares and information about over 1,000 possible rail and coach combinations.

- Bus travel in Paris is surprisingly easy, especially if you obtain (free of charge), one of the splendidly clear maps of Metro and bus routes (*une carte du réseau*) from any main-line Metro station or bus station. The routes are arranged logically, and you have the bonus of countless free mystery tours of Paris. A fuller guide, *Le Guide de Paris-Bus*, is available from news kiosks.

- See page 95 for information about cheap travel on the buses in Paris by means of a *carnet*, *Formule 1*, *carte jaune*, *carte orange* or *Paris-Sésame*.
  While you are making up your mind between these alternatives it is probably better to buy a *carnet* of 10 Metro-Autobus tickets from a Metro station or a bus terminus (you can share them with friends), than to buy single tickets, which are about twice as expensive. For convenience, choose either the *Paris-Sésame* or the *carte jaune*. But compare prices.

- **Bus routes** are divided into sections. If your journey covers 1 or 2 sections, you require 1 ticket for each journey. For 3 sections or more, you use up 2 tickets.

- **Punching your own ticket** (*composter*): when using ordinary tickets on the buses, you have to insert these as you enter into a small machine fitted behind the driver. This punches a hole in them, so that they cannot be used again.
  However, you MUST NOT PUNCH the *carte jaune*, *carte orange*, *Formule 1* or *Paris-Sésame* tickets on the buses, but simply show them to the driver.

I'd like a leaflet about excursions, please

Je voudrais un dépliant sur les excursions, s'il vous plaît
je voodreh uŋ daypleeahŋ sewr layz ehkskewrzyoŋ, seel voo pleh

Is there a bus or a coach for Paris tomorrow?

Est-ce qu'il y a un bus ou un car pour Paris demain?
ehskeelya uŋ bews oo uŋ kar poor paree demaŋ?

I'd like to book two seats

Je voudrais réserver deux places
je voodreh raysehrvay der plas

a single

un aller
un alay

a return

un aller-retour
un alay retoor

How much is that?

C'est combien?
seh koŋbyaŋ?

When do we arrive in Bordeaux?

On arrive à Bordeaux à quelle heure?
oŋ areev a bordoh a kehl err?

Where do we get on the bus?

Où est-ce qu'on prend le bus?
oo ehskoŋ prahŋ le bews?

Is the bus station near here?

Est-ce que la gare routière est près d'ici?
ehske la gar rootyehr eh preh deesee?

How often is there a bus?

Il y a un bus tous les combien?
eelya uŋ bews too lay koŋbyaŋ?

Where's the bus stop?

Où est l'arrêt, s'il vous plaît?
oo eh lareh, seel voo pleh?

Which bus stop does the bus/coach for Marseille leave from?

L'autobus/le car pour Marseille part de quel arrêt?
lohtobews/le kar poor marseh-y par de kehl areh?

Travel by air

- Write to Air France, 158 New Bond Street, London W1 (tel 01 499 8611) or phone them at Heathrow (tel 01 759 2311) for information about flights to all areas.
- Other flights are provided by British Airways, British Caledonian, Capitol Air, Pan American and TWA.
- Two important French airlines are Air Inter and Touraine Air Transport (TAT). Ask about reduced-price travel during off-peak periods. There may also be reductions for age or family travel.
- There are airports at Nice, Bordeaux, Toulouse and Lyons, as well as the two well-known Paris airports, Roissy-Charles de Gaulle and Orly.
- From Roissy-Charles de Gaulle airport there are buses to Paris, arriving fairly near the Champs-Elysées. During the rush hour there may be delays. There is also a rail service to the Gare du Nord and Châtelet-Les Halles.
- From Orly airport.there are buses to the Invalides and Montparnasse. Trains run to the Gare d'Austerlitz and Saint-Michel.
- It is also possible to shuttle between Roissy- Charles de Gaulle airport and Orly, even by helicopter if you so wish.
- There are excursions in charter aircraft from airports in the regions to places of historical and scenic interest.
- If you prefer helicopter travel, Map Travel (3 rue du Tournon, 75006 Paris tel (1) 634 16 18) offers luxury tours, including accommodation.

What flight must I get to go to Brussels?	Pour aller à Bruxelles je dois prendre quel vol? *poor alay a brewsehl je dwa prahŋdr kehl vol?*
What time is the next flight to London?	A quelle heure est le prochain vol pour Londres? *a kehl err eh le proshaŋ vol poor loŋdr?*

Do I have to change planes?	Est-ce qu'il faut changer d'avion?
	ehskeel foh shahŋjay davyoŋ?
Where (do I have to change planes)?	Où ça?
	oo sa?
From which airport?	De quel aéroport?
	de kehl a-ayropor?
From which air terminal?	De quel aérogare?
	de kehl a-ayrogar?
Where is the departure lounge?	Où se trouve la salle de départ?
	oo se troov la sal de daypar?
What is the departure time?	Quelle est l'heure de départ?
	kehl eh lerr de daypar?
Where is the duty-free shop?	Où se trouve le magasin hors-taxe?
	oo se troov le magazaŋ or tax?
Is the flight delayed?	Est-ce que le vol est en retard?
	ehske le vol ehtaŋ retar?
When do I have to check in?	Quand est-ce qu'il faut s'enregistrer?
	kahŋtehskeel foh sahŋrejeestray?
Is there a bus to the airport/town centre?	Y a-t-il un bus à l'aéroport/au centre-ville?
	yateel uŋ bews a la-ayropor/oh sahŋtr-veel?
I'd like a seat . . .	J'aimerais une place . . .
	jehmereh ewn plas . . .
. . . by the window	. . . à côté de la fenêtre
	a kohtay de la fnehtr
. . . in the aisle	. . . côté couloir
	kohtay koolwar
. . . at the back	. . . à l'arrière
	a laryehr

Travel on the Metro

- The booklets, cards and special tickets listed below will reduce your travel expenses in Paris. They may be obtained from all Metro stations, from bus termini, and in shops displaying the RATP or *Carte Orange* logo. The *Paris-Sésame* and *Formule 1* are also on sale at the Paris railway stations and RER stations. The RER (*Réseau Exprès Régional*) is the express Parisian suburban and underground line.

- The first four are particularly good value for the sightseer because they are for use interchangeably on Metro and bus within Paris and are very simple to use. (They are not for use on the RER, except when you buy a 'Paris-Sésame', but you can see most sights without needing to use the RER.)

- For the *carte jaune* and the *carte orange* you will need a passport-size photograph. It is simpler and cheaper to take one with you from Britain. You can get one at Victoria Station before catching the boat train if necessary.

  - a booklet (*carnet*) of 10 *Metro-Autobus* tickets.

  - a *Paris-Sésame*, valid from any date for 2, 4 or 7 days. Unlimited travel in 1st class on the Metro and RER, on the Montmartre funicular and on the whole bus network. Non-transferable. No photo needed.

  - a *carte jaune* (weekly pass), starting on Mondays. Unlimited travel on bus and Metro within the zones chosen (zones 1–2 are usually sufficient). If you arrive on a Saturday, you could buy a carnet of 10 tickets to share with a friend to last until Monday, when your *carte jaune* bacomes valid. The *carte jaune* looks like a *carte orange* at first sight, but differs from it by the coupon you buy to go with it. Non-transferable. Photo needed.

  - a *carte orange*. Similar to the *carte jaune*, but it is a monthly pass, starting on the first day of the month.

For the *Paris-Sésame*, *carte jaune*, and *carte orange*, simply show the card, containing (if necessary) your photo and the relevant ticket you have bought, as you enter the bus or Metro. *Don't* try to punch (*composter*) these as you would punch an ordinary *Metro-Autobus* ticket (see page 91). If you do so, you will not be able to use them again.

● a *Formule 1*: a 24-hour pass for use on the Metro, the RER, and suburban railway trains (but *not* on the buses). Ask for zones 1–2 (*zones un-deux*) if you wish to cover Paris only, zones 1, 2, 3 (*zones un, deux, trois*) – more expensive – if you wish to include the suburbs. Non-transferable.

● The *carte hebdomadaire*. You can take 2 trips daily up to a maximum of 12 journeys in a week, beginning on any day, but for the buses and the RER the journeys have to be made between two points determined in advance.

● For more detailed information, ask for the free brochure *RATP: Quel titre choisir?* where the tickets are sold. An English version is available.
● You can ask for a free plan (*un plan*) of the Metro when you buy your ticket.
● Each line (*ligne*) has two directions (*directions*). To find your direction, follow your line through on the map of the Metro from the station where you are, through the station you want to go to, to the end of the line. The last station on the line is the name of your direction.
Imagine you are at the Gare du Nord in the following diagram:

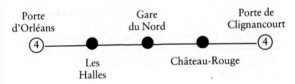

For Les Halles, you need *ligne 4, direction Porte d'Orléans*.
For Château-Rouge you need *ligne 4, direction Porte de Clignancourt*.

I'd like a booklet of tickets and a plan

Je voudrais un carnet de tickets et un plan
je voodreh uŋ karnay de teekay ay uŋ plahŋ

the automatic barrier

le portillon automatique
le porteeyoŋ otomateek

the (Metro) train

la rame
la ram

the (Metro) station

la station
la stasyoŋ

Is it necessary to change trains to get to Versailles?

Pour aller à Versailles faut-il changer de train?
poor alay a vehrsa-y fohteel shahŋjay de traŋ?

Which direction must I get?

Je dois prendre quelle direction?
je dwa prahŋdr kehl deerehksyoŋ?

Where must I get a connection?

Où faut-il prendre une correspondance?
oo fohteel prahŋdr ewn korehspoŋdahŋs?

You may see:	
Accès aux Quais	to the platforms
Entrée	entrance
Sortie	exit
Interdit de fumer	no smoking
Place reservée aux enceintes aux handicapés et aux mutilés de guerre	seat reserved for pregnant women, handicapped people and disabled ex-servicemen

SHOPPING

- Shops are generally open between 9 am and 5.30 pm or later, although post offices open at 8 am, and *boulangeries* at 7.30 or 8 am. Some hypermarkets do not close until 10 pm.
- Smaller shops often close during the lunch hour. Two hours is not uncommon, and in some parts lunch hours have been known to stretch to four hours. Many shops are closed on Mondays as well as Sundays.
- Butcher's shops: a *charcuterie* sells pork products, and a *boucherie* sells non-pork products.
- Stamps can be bought not only at the post offices, but also at the *tabacs*, which are easily spotted by the cigar-shaped sign outside.
- You can find high quality goods at very reasonable prices at the large stores such as **Prisunic**, **Mammouth** and **Casino**.

- French shopkeepers are usually very honest, but it is advisable to take care that you are not given change for 5 francs instead of 50 francs. If you do not have the correct change, it is safer to offer the nearest amount above the sum required rather than a large note.
- It is extremely expensive to develop films in France; you should wait until you return home.

I'm looking for . . .	Je cherche . . . *je shehrsh . . .*
I'm just looking	Je ne fais que regarder *je ne feh ke regarday*
Can you show me . . . ?	Pouvez-vous me montrer . . . ? *poovay voo me mo<u>ng</u>tray . . . ?*
Where do I pay?	Où se trouve la caisse? *oo se troov la kehs?*
Please write it down	Pouvez-vous l'écrire, s'il vous plaît? *poovay voo laykreer seel voo pleh?*
I don't want to spend more than . . .F	Je ne veux pas dépenser plus de . . .F *je ne ver pah daypah<u>ng</u>say plew de . . .frah<u>ng</u>*
Can I order it?	Est-ce que je peux le commander? *ehske je per le komah<u>ng</u>day?*
Do you accept credit cards?	Acceptez-vous les cartes de crédit? *aksehptay voo lay kart de kraydee?*
Can I pay by traveller's cheque?	Est-ce que je peux payer avec un chèque de voyage? *ehske je per payay avehk u<u>ng</u> shehk de vwayaj?*
Do I have to pay VAT?	Dois-je payer le TVA? *dwaj payay le tay vay ah?*

Where is the . . .	Où est . . . *oo eh . . .*
. . . baker's	. . . la boulangerie *la boolahŋjree*
. . . bookshop	. . . la librairie *la leebrehree*
. . . butcher's	. . . la boucherie *la booshree*
. . . cafe & tobacconist's	. . . le café-tabac *le kafay taba*
. . . confectioner's	. . . la pâtisserie *la pahteesree*
. . . chemist's/drugstore	. . . la pharmacie *la farmasee*
. . . dairy	. . . la crèmerie *la krehmree*
. . . delicatessen/pork butcher's	. . . la charcuterie *la sharkewtree*
. . . fish shop	. . . la poissonnerie *la pwasonree*
. . . fruiterer	. . . le marchand de fruits *le marshahŋ de frwee*
. . . grocer's	. . . l'alimentation/l'épicerie *laleemahŋtasyoŋ/* *laypeesree*
. . . newspaper kiosk	. . . le kiosque de journaux *le kyosk de joornoh*
. . . post office	. . . la poste *la post*
. . . self-service store	. . . le libre-service *le leebrsehrvees*
. . . shopping centre	. . . le centre commercial *le sahŋtr komehrsyal*

. . . stationer's	. . . la papeterie *la papaytree*
. . . supermarket	. . . le supermarché *le sewpehrmarshay*
. . . sweet shop	. . . la confiserie *la koŋfeezree*
. . . tobacconist's	. . . le bureau de tabac *le bewroh de taba*

Have you . . . , please?	Avez-vous . . . , s'il vous plaît? *avay voo . . . , seel voo pleh?*
How much is it?	C'est combien? *seh koŋbyaŋ?*
It's too expensive	C'est trop cher *seh troh shehr*
Haven't you any cheaper?	Vous n'en avez pas de moins cher? *voo nahŋ avay pah de mwaŋ shehr?*
I'll take it	Je le prends *je le prahŋ*
I'll have this one	Je prends celui-ci *je prahŋ selwee see*
I prefer that one	Je préfère celui-là *je prayfehr selwee la*
Will you gift-wrap it please?	Voulez-vous en faire un paquet-cadeau, s'il vous plaît? *voolay voo ahŋ fehr uŋ pakay kadoh, seel voo pleh?*
Are you open every day?	Vous ouvrez tous les jours? *vooz oovray too lay joor?*
That's all, thank you	C'est tout, merci *seh too mehrsee*
How much do I owe you?	Je vous dois combien? *je voo dwa koŋbyaŋ?*

Here's a 100-franc note	Voilà un billet de cent francs *vwala uŋ beeyeh de sahŋ* *frahŋ*
Excuse me, it's not right	Excusez-moi, ce n'est pas juste *ekskewzay mwa, sneh pah* *jewst*
I owe you . . .	Je vous dois . . . *je voo dwa . . .*
I gave you . . .	Je vous ai donné . . . *je vooz ay donay . . .*
You have to give me three francs change	Il faut me rendre trois francs *eel foh me rahŋdr trwa frahŋ*
But you gave me only two francs back	Mais vous ne m'avez rendu que deux francs. *meh voo ne mavay rahŋdew* *ke der frahŋ*

You may hear:

Vous désirez? *voo dayzeeray?*	Can I help you?
Voilà. Et avec ça? *vwala ay avehk sa?*	There you are. Anything else?
Lequel voulez-vous? *lekehl voolay voo?*	Which one do you want?
C'est tout? *seh too?*	Is that all?
Ça fait dix francs *sa feh dee frahŋ*	That's ten francs in all
Et voilà quatre francs que je vous rends *eh vwala katr frahŋ ke je voo rahŋ*	And there's four francs change
Voulez-vous que j'en fasse un paquet cadeau? *voolay voo ke jahŋ fas un pakay kadoh?*	Shall I gift wrap it?

General complaints

I want to complain about this	Je veux me plaindre de ceci *je ver me plandr de sesee*

It's too ...	Il est trop ... *eel eh troh ...*

... dark	... foncé *fonsay*
... expensive	... cher *shehr*
... light (in colour)	... clair *klehr*
... light (in weight)	... léger *layjay*
... narrow/tight	... étroit *aytrwa*
... wide	... large *larj*

This is shop-soiled	Ceci est défraîchi *sesee eh dayfrehshee*
This is broken	Ceci est cassé *sesee eh kassay*
Can you exchange this?	Pouvez-vous l'échanger? *poovay voo layshahnjay?*
I'd like a refund	Je voudrais me faire rembourser *je voodreh me fehr rahnboorsay*
Here's the receipt	Voici la quittance *vwasee la keetahns*
I bought it yesterday	Je l'ai acheté(e) hier *je lay ashtay eeyehr*
It was a present	C'était un cadeau *sayteh un kadoh*

At the department store

Excuse me, where's the department for . . . ?	Excusez-moi, où est le rayon de . . . ? *ehkskewzay mwa oo eh le rayon de . . . ?*
What floor is it on?	C'est à quel étage? *sehta kehl aytaj?*
It's on the ground floor	C'est au rez-de-chaussée *seht oh ray de shohsay*
It's on the first floor	C'est au premier étage *sehtoh premyehr aytaj*
second	deuxième *derzyehm*
third	troisième *trwazyehm*
fourth	quatrième *katryehm*
fifth	cinquième *saŋkyehm*

Is there a . . . ?	Est-ce qu'il y a . . . ? *ehkskeelya . . . ?*
Where is the . . . ?	Où est . . . ? *oo eh . . . ?*

. . . escalator	. . . un escalier roulant *uŋ ehskalyay roolahŋ*
. . . lift (elevator)	. . . un ascenseur *uŋ asahŋserr*
. . . cash desk	. . . la caisse *la kehs*
. . . staircase	. . . un escalier *uŋ ehskalyay*
. . . exit	. . . la sortie *la sortee*

10.

Buying clothes

Have you . . .	Avez-vous . . .
	avav voo . . .
. . . a bathing suit	. . . un maillot de bain
	un mayoh de ban
. . . a blouse	. . . un chemisier
	un shemeezyay
. . . a bra	. . . un soutien-gorge
	un sootyan gorj
. . . a cap	. . . un casquette
	ewn kaskeht
. . . a dress	. . . une robe
	ewn rob
. . . a handbag	. . . un sac à main
	un sak a man
. . . a hat	. . . un chapeau
	un shapoh
. . . some jeans	. . . un jean
	un jeen
. . . a jersey	. . . un tricot
	un treekoh
. . . a pullover	. . . un pull
	un pewl
. . . some pyjamas	. . . un pyjama
	un peejama
. . . a raincoat	. . . un imperméable
	un anpehrmayabl
. . . some shoes	. . . des chaussures
	day shohsewr
. . . some socks	. . . des chaussettes
	day shohseht
. . . some swimming trunks	. . . un maillot de bain
	un mayoh de ban

. . . a T-shirt	. . . un tee-shirt *uŋ tee shert*
. . . some tights	. . . un collant *uŋ kolahŋ*
. . . some trousers (pants)	. . . un pantalon *un pahŋtaloŋ*
. . . some underpants/panties	. . . un slip *uŋ sleep*

Size

What size are you?	Quelle taille portez-vous? *kehl tahy portay voo?*
I take size 12	Je porte du 38 *je port dew trahŋt weet*

Men's Suits and Overcoats

British	36	38	40	42	44	46	48	50
American	36	38	40	42	44	46	48	50
Continental	46	48	50/52	54	56	58/60	62	64

Men's Shirts

British	14	14½	15	15½	16	16½	17	17½
American	14	14½	15	15½	16	16½	17	17½
Continental	35	36/37	38	39/40	41	42/43	44	45

Men's Shoes

British	7	7½	8	8½	9	9½	10	10½	11
American	7½	8	8½	9	9½	10	10½	11	11½
Continental	41		42		43		44		45

Women's Dresses and Suits

British	8	10	12	14	16	18	20	22
American	–	8	10	12	14	16	18	20
Continental	–	36	38	40	42	44	46	48

Women's Shoes

British	4	4½	5	5½	6	6½	7	7½
American	5½	6	6½	7	7½	8	8½	9
Continental	36	37	38	38	39	40	41	41

I'd like a . . . dress	Je voudrais une robe . . . *je voodreh ewn rob . . .*
. . . cotton	. . . en coton *ahŋ kotoŋ*
. . . nylon	. . . en nylon *ahŋ neeloŋ*
. . . silk	. . . en soie *ahŋ swa*
. . . wool	. . . en laine *ahŋ lehn*
. . . leather	. . . en cuir *ahŋ kweer*
. . . linen	. . . en lin *ahŋ laŋ*

You may hear:

Je peux vous être utile? aider? *je per vooz ehtr ewteelr? ayday?*	Can I help you?
De quelle couleur? *de kehl koolerr?*	What colour?
Quelle est votre taille/ pointure? *kehl eh votr tahy/ pwahŋtewr?*	What size are you?
Le voulez-vous en coton ou en laine? *le voolay voo ahŋ kotoŋ oo ahŋ lehn?*	Do you want it in cotton or wool?
Et avec ça/autre chose? *ay avehk sa/ohtr shohz?*	Anything else?
En voici un à 200 francs *ahŋ vwasee uŋ a der sahŋ frahŋ*	Here's one at 200 francs.

Buying food and drink

● For other items of food and drink, see **Eating Out** section.

At the grocer's

a carton of yoghurt	un pot de yaourt *uŋ poh de yaoor*
a litre of milk	un litre de lait *uŋ leetr de leh*
a kilo of butter	un kilo de beurre *uŋ keeloh de berr*
six tomatoes	six tomates *see tomat*
two slices of ham	deux tranches de jambon *der trahŋsh de jahŋboŋ*
a packet of biscuits	un paquet de biscuits *uŋ pakay de beeskwee*
a jar of jam	un pot de confitures *uŋ poh de koŋfeetewr*
100 grammes of sweets	cent grammes de bonbons *sahŋ gram de boŋboŋ*
a dozen eggs	une douzaine d'oeufs *ewn doozehn der*

At the baker's

a loaf	un pain *uŋ paŋ*
a French stick (thick)	une baguette *ewn bageht*
a French stick (thin)	une ficelle *ewn feesehl*
four rolls	quatre petits pains *katr ptee paŋ*

At the fruitshop

a kilo of apples	un kilo de pommes *uŋ keeloh de pom*
some bananas	des bananes *day banan*
a bunch of grapes	une grappe de raisins *ewn grap de rehzaŋ*
some oranges	des oranges *dayz orahŋj*
half a kilo of peaches	un demi-kilo de pêches *uŋ demee keeloh de pehsh*
some ripe pears	des poires mûres *day pwar mewr*
some plums	des prunes *day prewn*
some strawberries	des fraises *day frehz*

● For vegetables, see 'Vegetables, rice and pasta' on page 43.

At the butcher's

a joint of beef	un rôti de boeuf *uŋ rohtee de berf*
some chicken	du poulet *dew pooleh*
some lamb	de l'agneau *de lanyoh*
two lamb chops	deux côtelettes *der kohtleht*
some liver	du foie *dew fwa*
some veal	du veau *dew voh*

Shopping

At the pork butcher's/delicatessen

four rashers of bacon	quatre tranches de lard *katr trahŋsh de lar*
three slices of ham	trois tranches de jambon *trwa trahŋsh de jahŋboŋ*
300g of cheese	300g de fromage *trwa sahŋ gram de fromaj*
some pork	du porc *dew por*
500g of salami	500g de saucisson *saŋ sahŋ gram de sohseesoŋ*
eight sausages	huit saucisses *wee sohsees*

At the fishmonger's

a crab	un crabe *uŋ krab*
some cod	de la morue *de la morew*
	du cabillaud *dew kabeeyoh*
a herring	un hareng *uŋ arahŋ*
a lobster	une langouste *ewn lahŋgoost*
	un homard *uŋ omar*
some mussels	des moules *day mool*
some oysters	des huîtres *day weetr*
some prawns	des crevettes roses *day kreveht rohz*
some salmon	du saumon *dew sohmoŋ*

some shrimps	des crevettes grises *day kreveht greez*
a sole	une sole *ewn sohl*
a trout	une truite *ewn trweet*
some tuna	du thon *dew toŋ*

Drinks

a bottle of. . .	une bouteille de. . . *ewn booteh-y de. . .*
a carton of. . .	un carton de. . . *uŋ kartoŋ de. . .*
a can of. . .	une boîte de. . . *ewn bwat de. . .*
apple juice	jus de pommes *jew de pom*
beer	bière *byehr*
Coca-cola	Coca-cola *kohka kohla*
gin	gin *uŋ jeen*
grape juice	jus de raisin *jew de rehsaŋ*
lager	bière blonde *byehr bloŋd*
lemon juice	jus de citron *jew de seetroŋ*
lemonade	limonade *leemonad*
milk	lait *leh*

orange juice	jus d'orange *jew dorahnj*
red wine	vin rouge *van rooj*
rosé wine	vin rosé *van rohzay*
white wine	vin blanc *van blahn*
whisky	whisky *un weeskee*
brandy	un cognac *un konyak*
port	un porto *un portoh*
rum	un rhum *un rom*
sherry	un sherry *un shayree*
vermouth	un vermouth *un vehrmoot*
vodka	une vodka *ewn vodka*
hot chocolate	un chocolat *un shokola*
tomato juice	un jus de tomates *un jew de tomat*
tonic	un Schweppes *un shwehps*
liqueur	une liqueur *ewn leekerr*
mineral water	l'eau minérale *loh minayral*
fizzy	gazeuse *gazerz*
still	non-gazeuse *non gazerz*

Photography

I'd like a film for this camera	J'aimerais une pellicule pour cet appareil *jehmereh ewn pehleekewl poor seht apareh-y*
black and white	en noir et blanc *ahŋ nwar ay blahŋ*
colour	en couleurs *ahŋ koolerr*
for slides	pour diapositives *poor deeapozeeteev*
24/36 exposures	24/36 poses *vaŋ katr/trahŋt see pohz*
How much do you charge for developing?	Combien coûte le développement? *koŋbyaŋ koot le dayvlopmahŋ?*
I want . . . . prints of this photo	Je voudrais . . . . copies de cette photo *je voodreh . . . kopee de seht fotoh*
matt/glossy finish	sur papier mat/brillant *sewr papyay mat/breeyahŋ*
When will the photos be ready?	Quand est-ce que les photos seront prêtes? *kahŋtehske lay fotoh seroŋ preht?*
I need batteries for this camera	Il me faut des piles pour cet appareil *eel me foh day peel poor seht apareh-y*
Can you repair this camera?	Pouvez-vous réparer cet appareil? *poovay voo rayparay seht apareh-y?*
The film/wind-on mechanism is jammed	Le film/le levier d'avancement est bloqué *le feelm/le levyay davahŋsmahŋ eh blokay*

- **Lost jewellery, camera, clothing, luggage:** you should report to the nearest police station, where you will have to describe the lost item in French. A copy of this report can be required if you are claiming for the loss with an insurance company. You can also try the local lost property office.
- **Lost credit cards** should be reported immediately to your bank according to the instructions given on issue, and also to the police.
- **Banks** are usually open from Monday to Friday 8.30 or 9 am to 4.30 or later. Sometimes the smaller branches close for lunch. Exchange bureaux are often open later.

  You can use Visa cards to withdraw cash from French banks. They can even be used in the cashpoint machines of certain banks: check with your bank before leaving. It is also possible to use traveller's cheques at hotels, travel agents and at some shops. However, the exchange rate is usually more

favourable at a bank. You should have your passport at hand when cashing a traveller's cheque.
- **The Post Office:** most post offices are open from 8 am to 7 pm on weekdays (often closed 12 noon–2 pm) and from 8 am to noon on Saturdays. The main post office at 52 rue du Louvre, 75001 Paris is open 24 hours daily.

  Letters can be sent *poste restante* to any French post office.

Lost property

Where's the lost property office (lost and found office)?	Où se trouve le bureau des objets trouvés? *oo se troov le bewroh dayz objay troovay?*
I've lost . . .	J'ai perdu . . . *jay pehrdew . . .*
. . . my handbag	. . . mon sac à main *moŋ sak a maŋ*
. . . my money	. . . mon argent *moŋ arjahŋ*
. . . my passport	. . . mon passeport *moŋ paspor*
. . . my suitcase	. . . ma valise *ma valeez*
. . . my wallet	. . . mon portefeuille *moŋ portfe-y*
. . . my umbrella	. . . mon parapluie *mon paraplwee*
. . . my ring	. . . ma bague *ma bag*

I lost it . . .	Je l'ai perdu . . . *je lay pehrdew . . .*
. . . this morning	. . . ce matin *se matan*
. . . today	. . . aujourd'hui *ohjoordwee*
. . . yesterday	. . . hier *ee-ehr*
. . . 3 days ago	. . . il y a 3 jours *eelya trwa joor*
My name's on it	Mon nom est marqué dessus *mon non eh markay desew*
It is . . .	Il (elle) est . . . *eel (ehl) eh . . .*
. . . black	. . . noir *nwar*
. . . dark blue	. . . bleu foncé *bler fonsay*
. . . light blue	. . . bleu clair *bler klehr*
. . . empty	. . . vide *veed*
. . . full	. . . plein *plan*
. . . green	. . . vert *vehr*
. . . (quite) large	. . . (assez) grand *asay grahn*
. . . long	. . . long *lon*

. . . narrow	. . . étroit
	aytrwa
. . . new	. . . neuf
	nerf
. . . rectangular	. . . rectangulaire
	rehktahŋgewlehr
. . . red	. . . rouge
	rooj
. . . round	. . . rond
	roŋ
. . . short	. . . court
	koor
. . . square	. . . carré
	karay
. . . white	. . . blanc
	blahŋ
. . . wide	. . . large
	. . . *larj*
. . . yellow	. . . jaune
	john
. . . made of gold	. . . en or
	ahn or
. . . made of leather	. . . en cuir
	ahŋ kweer
. . . made of metal	. . . en métal
	ahŋ maytal
. . . made of nylon	. . . en nylon
	ahŋ neeloŋ
. . . made of plastic	. . . en plastique
	ahŋ plasteek
. . . made of silver	. . . en argent
	ahn arjahŋ
. . . made of wood	. . . en bois
	ahŋ bwa

You may hear:

C'est pour quoi? *seh poor kwa?*	Can I help you?
Quand est-ce que vous l'avez perdu? *kahŋ ehske voo lavay pehrdew?*	When did you lose it?
Où est-ce que vous l'avez perdu? *oo ehske voo lavay pehrdew?*	Where did you lose it?
Qu'est-ce qu'il y avait dedans? *kehskeelyaveh dedahŋ?*	What was there inside?
Il (elle) est comment? *eel (ehl) eh komahŋ?*	What's it like?
Revenez demain, ou téléphonez *revenay demaŋ oo taylayfonay*	Come back tomorrow, or phone

At the bank or exchange bureau

Where is there an exchange bureau?	Je cherche un bureau de change *je shersh uŋ bewroh de shahnj*
I'd like to cash . . .	Je voudrais toucher . . . *je voodreh tooshay . . .*
. . . a traveller's cheque	. . . un chèque de voyage *uŋ shehk de vwayaj*
. . . two cheques of 100 francs	. . . deux chèques de 100 francs *der shehk de sahŋ frahŋ*
I'd like to change some pounds (dollars)	Je voudrais changer des livres (dollars) *je voodreh shahŋjay day leevr (dolar)*

117

What is the rate of exchange?	Quel est le taux du change? *kehl eh le toh dew shahnj?*
Please give me . . .	Donnez-moi . . . s'il vous plaît *donaymwa . . . seel vou pleh*
. . . notes	. . . des billets *day beeyay*
. . . small change	. . . de la monnaie *de la moneh*
Here is my passport	Voici mon passeport *vwasee mon paspor*
Here it is	Le voici *le vwasee*
Is it free?	C'est gratuit? *seh gratwee?*
Is it included?	C'est compris? *seh konpree?*

You may hear:

Vous avez votre passeport? *vooz avay votr paspor?*	Have you got your passport?
Vous voulez combien? *voo voolay konbyan?*	How much do you want?
Voulez-vous signer ici? *voolay voo seenyay eesee?*	Will you sign here?
Passez à la caisse *pasay a la kehs*	You must go to the cash desk
en grosses coupures *ahn grohs koopewr*	in large notes (bills)
en petites coupures *ahn pteet koopewr*	in small notes (bills)

account	le compte *le kont*
balance	le solde *le sold*
breakdown/detailed account	le décompte *le daykont*

cheque (personal)	le chèque *le shehk*
cheque book	le carnet de chèques *le karnay de shehk*
commission	la commission *la komeesyoŋ*
credit card	la carte de crédit *la kart de kraydee*
equivalent value	le contrevaleur *le koŋtrevalerr*
Eurocheques	des eurochèques *days errohshehk*
extra charge	le supplément *le sewplaymahŋ*
exchange rate	le taux de change *le toh de shahŋj*
foreign currency	des devises étrangères *day deveez aytrahŋjehr*
form	le bon/la fiche *le boŋ/la feesh*
mistake	une erreur *ewn ehrerr*
receipt	le reçu *le resew*
reduction	la réduction *la raydewksyoŋ*
telex	le télex *le taylehx*
total	le montant *le moŋtahŋ*
transfer	le virement *le veermahŋ*
to make a credit transfer	faire un virement *fehr uŋ veermahŋ*
traveller's cheque	le chèque de voyage *le shehk de vwayaj*

Post Office

I'm looking for ...	Je cherche ... *je shehrsh ...*
... the post office	... la poste *la post*
... a letter box (mailbox)	... une boîte à lettres *ewn bwat a letr*
... a phone booth	... une cabine téléphonique *ewn kabeen taylayfoneek*
How much is it to send ...?	C'est combien pour envoyer ...? *seh koŋbyaŋ poor* *ahŋvwayay ...?*
I'd like to send ...	Je voudrais envoyer ... *je voodreh ahŋvwayay ...*
... a letter	... une lettre *ewn lehtr*
... a parcel	... un colis *uŋ kolee*
... a postcard	... une carte-postale *ewn kart postal*
... a postal order	... un mandat postal *uŋ mahŋda postal*
... to Britain	... en Grande-Bretagne *ahŋ grahŋd bretanye*
... to Ireland	... en Irlande *ahn eerlahŋd*
... to the USA	... aux Etats-Unis *ohz aytaz ewnee*
... to Australia	... à l'Australie *a lostralee*

I would like . . .	Je voudrais . . . *je voodreh . . .*
. . . three 2F stamps	. . . trois timbres à deux francs *trwa tanbr a der frahn*
. . . ten 2F5 stamps	. . . dix timbres à deux francs cinquante *dee tanbr a der frahn sankahnt*
. . . one 50-centime stamp	. . . un timbre à cinquante centimes *an tanbr a sankahnt santeem*

Which counter?	Quel guichet? *kehl geeshay?*
I'd like a phonecard	Je voudrais une Telécarte *je voodreh ewn taylaykart*
Can you give me the directory, please?	Pouvez-vous me donner l'annuaire, s'il vous plaît? *poovay voo me donay lanewehr, seel voo pleh?*

You may hear:

Voilà. C'est tout? *vwala seh too?*	There you are. Is that all?
Il faut remplir cette fiche *eel foh rahnpleer seht feesh*	You have to fill out this form
Ça fait cinq francs vingt *sa feh sank frahn van*	That's 5F 20 altogether
Qu'est-ce qu'il y a dedans? *kehskeelya dedahn?*	What's inside?
C'est trop lourd *seh troh loor*	It's too heavy

Telephoning

- Special 'telephone offices' are available in major post offices, where the calls are controlled by operators whom you pay when the call is finished. At 52 rue du Louvre, Paris, you can find telephone directories for all countries.
- Street phone boxes are often vandalised and unusable, so it may be quicker to find a post office. Theoretically, unused coins are returned, but as the mechanism is not always working correctly, it is sensible to use 1F rather than 5F coins.
- Phone boxes are available to take coins and phone cards (*cartes téléphoniques*). Phone cards can be bought at *bureaux de tabac*.
- There are still phones in cafés, restaurants and post offices using tokens (*jetons*) which you can buy at the counter.
- It is wise to ask the rates if you are phoning abroad from an hotel or restaurant, as they are allowed to charge higher than normal rates.
- To give you the phone number 123 12 34, a French person would normally express the number as 'one hundred and twenty three, twelve, thirty four', so if you wish to be given the number in the English way, ask for the number *chiffre par chiffre*.

Hello!	Allô! *aloh!*
Can you help me, please?	Pouvez-vous m'aider, s'il vous plaît? *poovay voo mehday seel voo pleh?*
I'd like the international operator	Je voudrais le service international *je voodreh le sehrvees aŋtehrnasyonal*
Directory Enquiries, please	Renseignements, s'il vous plaît *rahŋsehnymahŋ seel voo pleh*

What's the dialling code for Britain/America?	Quel est l'indicatif de la Grande-Bretagne/des États Unis? *kehl eh laŋdeekateef de la grahŋd bretanye/dayz aytaz ewnee?*
I want extension . . . , please	Je voudrais l'interne . . . s'il vous plaît *je voodreh laŋtehrn . . . , seel voo pleh*
Is . . . there, please?	Est-ce que . . . est là, s'il vous plaît? *ehske . . . eh la, seel voo pleh?*
It's . . . speaking	C'est . . . à l'appareil *seh . . . a lapareh-y*
I'd like to reverse the charges	Je voudrais téléphoner en PCV *je voodreh taylayfonay ahŋ pay say vay*
I'm phoning to tell you my arrival time	Je téléphone pour te dire l'heure de mon arrivée *je taylayfon poor te deer lerr de moŋ areevay*

I'm expecting to arrive . . .	Je compte arriver . . . *je kohŋt areevay . . .*
. . . tomorrow	. . . demain *demaŋ*
. . . at . . . o'clock	. . . à . . . heures *a . . . err*
. . . this afternoon	. . . cet après-midi *seht apreh meedee*
. . . before six o'clock	. . . avant six heures *avahŋ seez err*
. . . next week	. . . la semaine prochaine *la smehn proshehn*

You may see

décrocher le combiné	lift the receiver
la fente	the slot
composer le numéro	dial the number
la tonalité	the dialling tone
raccrocher	to hang up

You may hear:

Quel numéro demandez-vous? *kehl newmayroh demahŋdayvoo?*	What number are you calling?
Ce n'est pas libre *se neh pah leebr*	The line's engaged
C'est de la part de qui? *seh de la par de kee?*	Who's speaking?
Il n'y a personne *eel nya pehrson*	There's no answer
Ne quittez pas *ne keetay pah*	Hold the line
à l'appareil *a lapareh-y*	speaking
en dérangement/en panne *ahŋ dayrahŋjmahŋ/ahŋ pan*	out of order
Combien d'unités? *koŋbyaŋ dewneetay?*	How many units (phonecard)?
avec préavis *avehk prayavee*	person-to-person
PCV *pay say vay*	reverse charge call
Vous vous êtes trompé(e) de numéro *voo voozeht troŋpay de newmayroh*	You've got a wrong number

Cleaning and repairs

- Dry cleaning prices are relatively expensive, and the time taken may be 24 hours.

I'm looking for . . .	Je cherche . . . *je shehrsh . . .*
. . . a dry cleaner's	. . . une teinturerie *ewn taŋtewreree*
. . . an electrician	. . . un électricien *uŋ aylehktreesyaŋ*
. . . a garage mechanic	. . . un garagiste *uŋ garajeest*
. . . a laundrette	. . . une laverie automatique *ewn lavree otomateek*
. . . a plumber	. . . un plombier *uŋ plohŋbyay*
. . . a repair shop	. . . un atelier de réparations *aŋ atelyay de rayparasyoŋ*
. . . a shoe repairer	. . . un cordonnier *uŋ kordonyay*

It isn't working	Ça ne marche pas *sa ne marsh pah*
It has broken down	Il (elle) est en panne *eel (ehl) eht ahŋ pan*
It's torn	Il (elle) est déchiré *eel (ehl) eh daysheeray*
Can you repair my watch?	Est-ce que vous pouvez réparer ma montre? *ehske voo poovay rayparay ma moŋtr?*
How much is it to dry clean my sweater?	C'est combien pour nettoyer à sec mon tricot? *seh koŋbyaŋ poor netwayay a sehk moŋ treekoh?*

How long will you take to wash the clothes?	Vous allez mettre combien de temps à laver les vêtements? *vooz alay mehtr koŋbyaŋ de tahŋ a lavay lay vehtmahŋ?*
When will it be ready?	Quand est-ce qu'il sera prêt? *kahŋt ehskeel sera preh?*
How long will it take?	Ça va demander combien de temps? *sa va demahŋday koŋbyaŋ de tahŋ?*
Will it be long?	On en a pour longtemps? *on ahn a poor loŋtahŋ?*

I need a . . .	Il me faut . . . *eel me foh . . .*
. . . bicycle pump	. . . une pompe *ewn pohŋp*
. . . fuse	. . . un plomb/un fusible *uŋ plohŋ/uŋ fewzeebl*
. . . needle	. . . une aiguille *ewn aygweey*
. . . thread	. . . un fil *uŋ feel*
. . . repair kit	. . . une trousse de réparation *ewn troos de rayparasyoŋ*
. . . screwdriver	. . . un tournevis *uŋ toornevees*

It's fused	Il y a un plomb de sauté *eelya uŋ plohŋ de sohtay*
It needs heeling	Il est éculé *eel eht aykewlay*
to heel a shoe	remettre un talon *remehtr uŋ taloŋ*
to put a sole on a shoe	ressemeler un soulier *resemlay uŋ soolyay*

Information

Where's the information bureau?	Où se trouve le syndicat d'initiative? *oo se troov le sandeeka deeneesyateev?*
I should like some information about . . .	Je voudrais me renseigner sur . . . *je voodreh me rahnsehnyay sewr . . .*
. . . boarding houses	. . . les pensions *lay pahnsyon*
. . . camp sites	. . . les campings *lay kahnpeen*
. . . castles	. . . les châteaux *lay shahtoh*
. . . excursions	. . . les excursions *layz ehxkewrzyon*
. . . exhibitions	. . . les expositions *layz ehxpozeesyon*
. . . evening amusements	. . . les divertissements dans la soirée *lay deevehrteesmahn dahn la swaray*
. . . hotels	. . . les hôtels *layz ohtehl*
. . . monuments	. . . les monuments historiques *lay monewmahn eestoreek*
. . . museums	. . . les musées *lay mewzay*
. . . shows	. . . les spectacles *lay spehktakl*
. . . sports facilities	. . . les équipements sportifs *layz aykeepmahn sporteef*

Services

Have you . . .	Avez-vous . . .
	avay voo . . .
. . . some brochures	. . . quelques brochures
	kehlke broshewr
. . . some leaflets	. . . quelques dépliants
	kehlke daypleeahɲ
. . . a list of hotels	. . . une liste des hôtels
	ewn leest dayz ohtehl
. . . a map of the town	. . . une carte de la ville
	ewn kart de la veel
. . . a town plan	. . . un plan de la ville
	uɲ plahɲ de la veel

Can one/we/you . . . ?	Est-ce qu'on peut . . . ?
	ehskoɲ per . . . ?
. . . hire . . .	. . . louer . . .
	looay . . .
. . . visit . . .	. . . visiter . . .
	veezeetay . . .
. . . go there every day	. . . y aller tous les jours
	ee alay too lay joor

Useful questions

Where is . . . ?	Où se trouve . . . ?
	oo se troov . . . ?
When does it begin?	Ça commence à quelle heure?
	sa komahɲs a kehl err?
When does it end	Ça finit à quelle heure?
	sa feenee a kehl err?
How much does it cost?	Ça coûte combien?
	sa koot koɲbyaɲ?
What's the price of . . . ?	Quel est le prix de . . . ?
	kehl eh le pree de . . . ?

ESSENTIAL INFORMATION

Numerals

1	un	*un*	20	vingt	*van*	
2	deux	*der*	30	trente	*trahnt*	
3	trois	*trwa*	40	quarante	*karahnt*	
4	quatre	*katr*	50	cinquante	*sankahnt*	
5	cinq	*sank*	60	soixante	*swasahnt*	
6	six	*sees*	70	soixante-dix	*swasahnt dees*	
7	sept	*set*	80	quatre-vingts	*katr van*	
8	huit	*weet*	90	quatre-vingt-dix	*katr van dees*	
9	neuf	*nerf*	100	cent	*sahn*	
10	dix	*dees*	200	deux cents	*der sahn*	

Days of the week

Sunday	dimanche *deemahnsh*	**Thursday**	jeudi *jerdee*
Monday	lundi *lundee*	**Friday**	vendredi *vahndredee*
Tuesday	mardi *mardee*	**Saturday**	samedi *samdee*
Wednesday	mercredi *mehrkredee*		

Months

January	janvier *jahŋvyay*	**July**	juillet *jweeyeh*
February	février *fayvreeay*	**August**	août *oot*
March	mars *mars*	**September**	septembre *sehptahŋbr*
April	avril *avreel*	**October**	octobre *oktobr*
May	mai *meh*	**November**	novembre *novahŋbr*
June	juin *jwaŋ*	**December**	décembre *daysahŋbr*

Road information

- You can obtain a free brochure giving advice about driving abroad by phoning the AA or RAC (whether you are a member or not). This advice includes information about vehicle insurance (including Green Cards), lights, mirrors, nationality plates, age limits, police fines (which can be immediate and extremely high), seat belts, snow chains, warning triangles, hazard warning lights, etc. If you purchase insurance you receive also more detailed information which includes a selection of continental road signs, a table covering the speed limits in various countries, and detailed advice on emergency services.

Useful road signs

priority road
(even if there are no other signs)

end of priority road
(usually on entering urban zone)

intersection with priority to the right

give way at intersection

give way at roundabouts

priority to users of the main road

uneven road

no parking

entry prohibited

lane for slow vehicles

switch on headlights

halt for Customs post

halt for toll booth

speed limit 110 km per hour
(unless otherwise indicated)

level crossing with automatic barriers

tourist information centre

maximum speed 60 km/h

end of prohibition
(ie you MAY exceed
60 km/h)

minimum speed 30 km/h

end of minimum speed
zone

Remember   *RAPPEL*

Detour   *DÉVIATION*

Road closed   *ROUTE BARRÉE*

- **Parking:** large towns have the usual car parks and
  parking meters. However, smaller towns may have a
  system whereby you display a blue disc (*un disque de
  contrôle*) in the Blue Zones (*Zones Bleues*). This is
  obtainable free from Tourist Offices, garages or
  tobacconists. On it you indicate the time you parked.
  You are allowed one hour between 9–12.30 and
  14.30–19.00.
  The side of the street on which you may park varies,
  so it is best to imitate the local drivers.
- **Driving licence, registration and insurance papers:**
  up-to-date documents for these must be taken with
  you on holiday, and be readily available for the
  police. A valid British driving licence will suffice in
  France, but if you intend to travel in other countries,
  it may be advisable to obtain an International
  Driving Permit, details of which are available from
  British motoring organisations such as the AA and
  RAC.

- **Insurance:** although insurance policies issued in the UK and the Republic of Ireland automatically provide minimum cover in EEC countries, the overseas cover will satisfy only the minimum legal requirement, and it is quite possible that your cover will be less than in the UK. It is therefore advisable to consult your insurer, who will issue an International Green Card to extend your UK cover.
- If you are travelling through France to Spain, it is worth asking your insurer about a Bail Bond.
- Basic 3rd party insurance cover is available at the main frontier posts.
- **Car hire:** for this you need your driving licence and passport. The minimum age varies between 23 and 25.
- The SNCF (French Railways) will give you details about car hire combined with rail travel. Ask at your travel agency, write to the Bureau Central des Réservations, 3 rue Bernouilli, 75008 Paris or phone (16) 05 05 05 11 free of charge.
- Alternatively, ask at the local French railway station for *un pliant sur la location de voitures*. It is possible to hire a car in advance to await your arrival at your train desination.
- **Speed limits**

	normal weather	rain or poor visibility
autoroutes	130 km/hour (80 mph) (in urban sections it may be less)	110 km/hour (68 mph)
dual carriageways	110 km/h (68 mph)	100 km/h (62 mph)
other roads	90 km/h (56 mph)	80 km/h (50 mph)
towns	60 km/h (37 mph)	60 km/h (37 mph)

- **Tolls** (*péage*): the autoroutes (prefixed A on the road signs) are toll-operated except for their urban sections. This means you must be ready to halt and

133

pay the appropriate charge (in French currency)
shortly after you see a sign such as

   OR

either by paying the attendant or by throwing the
correct money into a special collection net. Certain
credit cards including Visa are now accepted on
French autoroutes. The cost may seem high, eg about
£33 for a single journey from Calais to Nice for a car
without caravan.

- The toll-booths can supply free maps of less crowded
roads, which do not require tolls. Some English
motoring organisations offer similar maps, or
recommended routes specially prepared to your own
requirements.
- **Accidents:** in case of a minor accident in France, it is
usually sufficient to fill in a standard accident form
(*un constat*). Each driver signs the other's copy. If
you cannot read French, and don't know what you
are signing, it is safer to call in the police, as you must
in the case of a major accident.

Emergencies

The British Consulate should be used only as a last
resort: police/insurance companies etc should be
contacted first. Remember to make a separate list of
credit card/passport numbers, and to keep a note of
emergency telephone numbers in case of theft.

Emergency telephone numbers

	France	Belgium	Switzerland
Fire	18	900	118
Ambulance	17	900	117
Police	17	901	117

Electricity

In most areas, this is the same voltage as Britain (220V), but the power points are different, and you need a special adaptor (available in Britain).

Belgium and Switzerland

French is spoken in both these countries, but there are some practical differences:

- In Belgium shops tend to close at 6 pm. In Switzerland they close at 6.30 pm Monday to Friday, and at 5 pm on Saturdays.
- Although the currency in all three countries is divided into francs and centimes (1F = 100 centimes), they are not interchangeable as they have different values.
- Motorways are toll-free in Belgium. In Switzerland you have to display a special motorway tax sticker. This costs about 30 Swiss francs and is available in Britain through the motoring organisations.
- Post Offices are recognisable by the *PTT* signs in Switzerland and by *Postes/Posterijen* in Belgium. You cannot make telephone calls or send telegrams from Belgian Post Offices: for this you have to look for a special *Téléphone/Télégraphe* office. Swiss postboxes, like the French ones, are yellow. The Belgian ones are red.

Conversion tables

Distance eg 10 km = 6 miles, 10 miles = 16 km

miles	6	12	19	25	31	37	44
km/mile	10	20	30	40	50	60	70
km	16	32	48	64	80	97	113

miles	50	56	62	68	75	81	
km/mile	80	90	100	110	120	130	
km	129	145	161	177	194	210	

Temperature

°F	0	20	32	50	70	87	98.6	105	212
°C	−18	−3	0	10	21	30	36.9	40	100

Liquids

litres		5	10	15	20	25
imperial gallons		1.1	2.2	3.3	4.4	5.5
US gallons		1.3	2.6	3.9	5.2	6.5

litres		30	35	40	45	50
imperial gallons		6.6	7.7	8.8	9.9	11.0
US gallons		7.8	9.1	10.4	11.7	13.0

Weights eg. 1 kg = 2.2 lbs, 1 lb = 0.46 kg

lbs	1.1	2.2	4.4	6.6	8.8	11.0
kg/lb	½	1	2	3	4	5
kg	0.23	0.46	0.92	1.38	1.84	2.3

lbs	13.2	15.4	17.6	19.8	21.0
kg/lb	6	7	8	9	10
kg	2.76	3.22	3.68	4.14	4.6

NB 1000 g = 1 kg

WORD LIST

Note:
For numerals, see page 129
m = masculine, f = feminine

A
abbey une abbaye
to be able pouvoir
about/roughly environ
above au-dessus (de)/en haut
abroad à l'étranger
abscess un abscès
absent absent
to accept accepter
accident un accident
account le compte
accurate exact/correct
ache une douleur
in addition en plus
address une adresse
admission l'entrée (f)
to admit laisser entrer
adult un(e) adulte
in advance en avance
advertisement une annonce
aeroplane un avion
after après/au bout de
afternoon un après-midi
afternoon performance la matinée
aftershave (lotion) une lotion après-rasage
again encore/de nouveau
age un âge
agency une agence
air l'air (m)
  by air par avion
  air bed le matelas pneumatique
  air conditioned climatisé/air conditionné
  airmail par avion
  airport un aéroport
  air sick le mal de l'air
  air terminal un aérogare
  open air en plein air
all/every tout
  all year toute l'année
allergy une allergie
allowed permis
also aussi

always toujours
amazing incroyable
ambulance une ambulance
America l'Amérique (f)
American américain
amount la quantité/la somme (money)
amusements les divertissements (m)
amusing amusant/drôle
anchovies les anchois (m)
animal un animal
ankle la cheville
anorak un anorak
antibiotic un antibiotique
antiques les antiquités (f)
antiseptic antiseptique
anything quelque chose/n'importe quoi
appetizing appétissant
apple la pomme
  apple juice le jus de pommes
appliance un appareil
appointment le rendez-vous
approximately à peu pres
apricot un abricot
April avril
architect un architecte
area (part of town) un quartier
  (part of country) une région
around autour (de)
  all around tout autour
arrival une arrivée
to arrive arriver
art art (m)
  art gallery une galerie d'art
article/item un article
as/like comme
ashtray le cendrier
to ask (for) demander
asparagus les asperges (f)
aspirin l'aspirine (f)
assistant un employé

137

asthma l'asthme (m)
athletics l'athlétisme (m)
attack/fit la crise
attendant
  petrol attendant le pompiste
August août
automatic automatique
average moyen(ne)
away
  a long way away loin
  go away! allez-vous en!
awful affreux (-euse)/ moche/terrible

B
baby le bébé
baby food les aliments (m) pour bébés
bachelor le célibataire
back le dos
  at the back à l'arrière
  backache le mal de reins
bacon le lard
  bacon and eggs les oeufs (m) au bacon
bad mauvais
badly mal
bag le sac
baggage/bags les bagages (m)
baked au four
baker's la boulangerie
balance (money) le solde
balcony le balcon
ball (toy) le ballon
  (dance) la balle
ballet le ballet
ball-point pen le stylo (à bille)
banana la banane
bandage le pansement
bank la banque
bank note le billet de banque
bar le bar
Barclaycard/Visa la carte bleue
barmaid la serveuse
barrier (automatic) le portillon automatique
bath le bain/la baignoire

to have a bath prendre un bain
to bathe se baigner
bathroom la salle de bains
battery
  car battery la batterie
to be être/se trouver
beach la plage
bean le haricot
  green beans les haricots verts
beard la barbe
beautiful beau (belle)
because parce que/car
bed le lit
  bed and breakfast chambre avec petit déjeuner
  bedroom la chambre
bee une abeille
beef le boeuf/ le rosbif
beer la bière
beetroot le betterave
before (time) avant
  (place) devant
to begin commencer
beginning le début
behind derrière/en arrière
Belgian belge
Belgium Belgique
bell (church) la cloche
  (electric) la sonnette
below en bas
belt la ceinture
  safety belt la ceinture de sécurité
bend (in road) le virage
beret le béret
beside à côté de
better meilleur
bicycle le vélo/la bicyclette
  by bicycle en vélo
  bicycle pump la pompe
bidet le bidet
big (fat) gros(se)
  (tall) grand
bill la note/l'addition (f)
bindings les fixations (f)
bird un oiseau
birthdate la date de naissance
birthday un anniversaire

happy birthday! bon anniversaire!
biro le stylo
biscuit le biscuit
black noir
blanket la couverture
block (of flats) un immeuble
blood le sang
  (high) blood pressure la tension (élevée)
blouse le chemisier
blown (fuse/light bulb) sauté
blue bleu
board
  full board la pension complète
  half board la demi-pension
boarding house la pension
boat le bateau
  by boat en bateau/par le bateau
body le corps
boiled (potatoes) nature, vapeur
bomber jacket le blouson
to book/reserve réserver/retenir
book le livre
booking/réservation la réservation
booklet le carnet
boot (of car) le coffre
  (footwear) la botte
boring ennuyeux (-euse)
to borrow emprunter
boss le patron/la patronne
bottle la bouteille
bottom (far end) le fond
boulevard le boulevard
bowl le bol
box la boîte
boxing la boxe
boy le garçon
bra le soutien-gorge
brake le frein
brave/courageous courageux (-euse)
bread le pain/la baguette
to break casser
  to break down être en panne/tomber en panne
breakdown (mechanical) la panne
breakfast le petit déjeuner
bridge le pont
briefs/pants le slip/la culotte
to bring apporter
Britain la Grande-Bretagne
Brittany la Bretagne
British britannique
broadcast/programme une émission
broken down/not working en panne
brother le frère
brown brun/marron
brush la brosse
Brussels Bruxelles
buffet le buffet
building le bâtiment
bulb une ampoule
to burgle cambrioler
burnt brûlé
burst (tyre) crevé
bus un autobus/un bus
  by bus en bus/en autobus
  bus station la gare routière
  bus stop un arrêt
butcher's la boucherie
  pork butcher's la charcuterie
butter le beurre
button le bouton
to buy acheter

C
cabbage le chou
cake le gâteau
  cake shop la pâtisserie
calculator le calculateur de poche
calf le veau
to call appeler
  to call back rappeler
  to make a reverse-charge call téléphoner en PCV

call (on phone) le coup de téléphone
calm calme
calor gas le butane
    calor gas store le dépôt de butane
camera un appareil (photo)
to camp camper
    camp bed le lit de camp
    camp site le camping/le terrain de camping
camper le campeur
camping equipment le matériel de camping
can la boîte
Canada le Canada
    in/to Canada au Canada
Canadian canadien
to cancel annuler
canteen la cantine
car une auto/une voiture
    car hire la location de voitures
    car hire agency l'agence (f) de location de voitures
    car park le parking
    car sick
        I am car sick j'ai le mal de la route
carafe la carafe
caravan la caravane
card la carte
    banker's card la carte bancaire
    credit card la carte de crédit
    to play cards jouer aux cartes
careful
    be careful! attention!
caretaker le/la concierge
carriage la voiture
to carry/wear porter
carton (of cigarettes) la cartouche
    (of yoghurt) le pot
    (of milk) le carton
cartoon le dessin animé
case la valise
to cash a cheque toucher/encaisser un chèque

cash l'argent (m)/la liquide
cashdesk la caisse
cassette la cassette
    cassette recorder le magnétophone
castle le château
cathedral la cathédrale
Catholic catholique
cauliflower le chou-fleur
cellar la cave
centime le centime
centimetre le centimètre
centre le centre
    town centre le centre-ville
    shopping centre le centre commercial
certain certain
certainly certainement
chain la chaîne
chair la chaise
to change changer
change la monnaie
channel (on TV) la chaîne
    (English) Channel la Manche
charge le prix/le tarif
extra charge le supplément
cheap bon marché
cheaper moins cher
to check vérifier
check-out la caisse
cheese le fromage
chemist's (drugstore) la pharmacie
cheque le chèque
    cheque book le carnet de chèques
    traveller's cheque le chèque de voyage
cherry la cerise
chewing gum le chewing-gum
chicken le poulet
child un(e) enfant
chips les frites (f)
chocolate le chocolat
    bar of chocolate la plaque de chocolat
choice le choix
to choose choisir
chop la côtelette
Christmas Noël (m)

church une église
cider le cidre
cigarette la cigarette
  cigarette case un étui à
    cigarettes
cine-camera la caméra
cinema le cinéma
circle (in theatre) le balcon
circus le cirque
class la classe
  first class première classe
  second class seconde
    classe
to clean nettoyer
  to have something
    cleaned faire nettoyer
clean propre
cliff la falaise
climbing/
    mountaineering l'alpi-
      nisme (m)
clinic la clinique
clock une horloge
to close fermer
closed fermé
cloth (fabric) le tissu
  (duster) le torchon
clothes les vêtements (m)
  sports clothes la tenue de
    sport
club le club
  youth club la maison des
    jeunes
clutch un embrayage
coach (railway) le wagon/la
    voiture
  (bus) un car
  by coach en car
coast la côte
coat le manteau
coca-cola le coca-cola
cod le cabillaud/la morue
coeducational mixte
coffee le café
  (white) café au lait
  (with cream) café-crème
  (black) café nature
coffee pot la cafetière
coin la pièce
cold froid
  to have a cold avoir un
    rhume/être enrhumé

I am cold j'ai froid
collection la collection
  (of post) la levée
collision la collision
colour la couleur
to come venir
comedy (film) un film
    comique
comfortable confortable
commission la commission
compact disc le disque
    compact
compartment le
    compartiment
to complain faire une
    réclamation/se plaindre
complaint la réclamation
complete complet
compulsory obligatoire
computer le calculateur/
    l'ordinateur
  computer games les jeux
    d'ordinateur
concert le concert
confectioner's la confiserie
congratulations! félici-
    tations!
connection (in Metro) la
    correspondance
constipated constipé
consulate le consulat
consulting room la salle de
    consultation
convenient commode
to cook faire la cuisine
cook le chef
cooked cuit
  well cooked bien cuit
cooker la cuisinière
corkscrew le tire-bouchon
corn (food) le maïs
  (on foot) le cor
corner le coin
correct exact/correct
corridor le corridor
to cost coûter
cost le prix/le tarif
costume le costume
  bathing costume le
    maillot de bain
cotton
  made of cotton en coton 141

cotton wool le coton hydrophile/l'ouate
couchette la couchette
to cough tousser
cough drops les pastilles (f) contre la toux
council flat un HLM
counter le guichet
(in shop) le rayon/le comptoir
country le pays
countryside la campagne
course le cours
cover charge le couvert
crab le crabe
crayfish les écrevisses (f)
cream la crème
credit le crédit
credit card la carte de crédit
cricket le cricket
crisps les chips (m)
cross la croix
crossing
    sea crossing la traversée
    level crossing le passage à niveau
    pedestrian crossing le passage (pour piétons)
crossroads le carrefour
cup la tasse
currency (foreign) les devises étrangères (f)
customs la douane
    customs duty la taxe/les droits de douane
to cut couper
cyclist le/la cycliste

D
daily quotidien(ne)
dairy la crèmerie
danger le danger
dangerous dangereux (-euse)
to dance danser
dance le bal
dark (of colour) foncé
    (of sky) noir
date la date
daughter la fille
day le jour/la journée

the day before la veille, avant-hier
the next day le lendemain
the day after tomorrow après-demain
dead mort
to deal with s'occuper de
December décembre
deck chair la chaise longue/le transat
to declare déclarer
    nothing to declare rien à déclarer
deep profond
delay le retard
delayed en retard
delicatessen la charcuterie
dentist le/la dentiste
deodorant le déodorant
department le département/le rayon
departure gate la porte de départ
departure lounge la salle de départ
departure time l'heure de départ
to depend dépendre
    that depends ça dépend
deposit la caution
desk (= cashdesk) la caisse
dessert le dessert
destination la destination
diabetic diabétique
to dial composer le numéro
    to dial 999 appeler police-secours
    dialling code l'indicatif (m)
    dialling tone la tonalité
diarrhoea la diarrhée/la colique
diesel (oil) le gas-oil
to dine dîner
dining room la salle à manger
diploma le brevet/le certificat/le diplôme
direction le sens/la direction
    all directions toutes directions

directory un annuaire
dirty sale
disco la disco(thèque)
  to go to a disco aller en boîte
dish le plat
distance la distance
distant/far away loin/éloigné
diversion la déviation
divorced divorcé
dizzy spells des vertiges (f)
to do faire
doctor le docteur/le médecin
documentary le documentaire
dog le chien
door la porte
  (of car) la portière
dormitory le dortoir
dozen la douzaine
to doubt douter
doubt la doute
  no doubt sans doute
Dover Douvres
drawing le dessin
dress la robe
to drink boire
drink la boisson
drinkable (of water) potable
  (non-)drinking water eau (non) potable
to drive conduire/rouler
drive la randonnée
driver le chauffeur/le conducteur
drunk ivre
to dry clean nettoyer à sec
dry cleaning/dry cleaner's le nettoyage à sec
dubbed doublé
  dubbed in French en version française
duration la durée
dust la poussière
dustbin la poubelle
Dutch hollandais

E
each chaque

each person/day/night par personne/jour/nuit
each (one) chacun(e)
ear une oreille
early de bonne heure
to earn/win gagner
east l'est (m)
Easter Pâques (f.pl)
easy facile
to eat manger
economics l'économie (f)
to economise économiser
edge le bord
Edinburgh Edimbourg
education l'enseignement (m)/l'éducation (f)
effort un effort
  it's not worth the effort ce n'est pas la peine
egg un oeuf
elbow le coude
eldest aîné
electric électrique
electrician un électricien
electricity l'électricité (f)
elegant élégant
emergency une urgence
emergency exit la sortie de secours
employee un(e) employé(e)
employer un employeur
empty vide
end la fin/le bout
  at the end of au bout de
energy l'énergie (f)
engaged (number/seat/toilet) occupé
  (of taxi) pris/pas libre
  (betrothed) fiancé
engagement les fiançailles (f)
engine le moteur
England l'Angleterre (f)
English anglais(e)
to enjoy oneself s'amuser
enjoy your meal! bon appétit!
enough assez
  that's enough ça suffit!
to enrol s'inscrire
to enter entrer

143

entertainment la distraction
entirely entièrement/complètement/tout à fait/totalement
entrance une entrée
entrance fee le prix d'entrée
entry
no entry défense d'entrer
envelope une enveloppe
epileptic épileptique
equal/the same égal
equivalent value le contrevaleur
error une erreur
escalator un escalier roulant
espresso coffee un express
essential essentiel (-elle)
Eurocheques des Eurochèques (m)
Europe l'Europe (f)
European européen
even même
evening le soir/la soirée
in the evening le soir/en soirée
good evening! bonsoir!
every tout/chaque
everybody tout le monde
everywhere partout
exact juste/exact
exactly exactement
to exaggerate exagérer
example un exemple
to exceed excéder/dépasser
excellent excellent
except (for) sauf/à part/à l'exception de
excess fare/excess charge le supplément
to exchange échanger/changer
exchange un échange
exchange bureau le bureau de change
exchange rate (at today's price) le cours du change (au cours du jour)
excursion une excursion
excuse me! excusez-moi/pardon!

exhibition une exposition
to exist exister
exit la sortie
emergency exit la sortie de secours
to expect compter
expenditure la dépense
expenses les frais (m)
expensive cher (chère)
not very expensive pas très cher
to explain expliquer
expression/phrase une expression
extension (phone) le poste
extra en plus/supplémentaire
extraordinary extraordinaire
extremely extrêmement
eye un oeuil (pl yeux)

F
face la figure/le visage
face flannel le gant de toilette
facing en face de/faisant face à
factory une usine
fair (hair) blond
false faux (fausse)
family la famille
famous célèbre
far (from) loin (de)
as far as jusqu'à
fare le prix du billet
at normal fare à tarif normal
at reduced fare à tarif réduit
fare stage la section
farm la ferme
father le père
father-in-law le beau-père
February février
to feel (se) sentir
ferry le ferry
by ferry en ferry
festival (musical) le festival
fiancé le fiancé/la fiancée

field le champ
to fight se battre
to fill (in) remplir
  to fill up with petrol faire
    le plein
fillet le filet
film (for camera) la pellicule
  (in cinema) le film
to find trouver
fine (penalty) la
    contravention/une
    amende
  (weather) beau
  (OK) bien/d'accord
finger le doigt
to finish finir
fire! au feu!
fireman le (sapeur-)pompier
first premier (-ère)
first of all d'abord
fish le poisson
fishing la pêche
fitted out aménagé
to fix fixer/arranger/réparer
fixed-price menu le menu à
    prix fixe
flash le flash
flat un appartement
flats (blocks of) un
    immeuble
flavour le parfum
flight le vol
floor (= storey) un étage
  (= boards) le plancher/le
    parquet
  ground floor le rez-de-
    chaussée
  on the floor par terre
flower la fleur
'flu la grippe
fog/mist le brouillard/la
    brume
to follow suivre
food les provisions (f)
  sea food les fruits de mer
    (m)
food store une alimentation
foot le pied
  on foot à pied
football le football
footpath le sentier/le
    chemin

for pour
  (= because) car
forbidden interdit/défendu
  it is forbidden
    to... défense de...
foreign étranger (-ère)
forest la forêt
to forget oublier
to forgive pardonner/
    excuser
  forgive me excusez-moi
fork la fourchette
form la fiche, le bon
  order form le bon de
    commande
formula le formulaire
franc le franc
France la France
free libre/gratuit
freezer le congélateur
French français(e)
Friday vendredi
fried potatoes pommes
    frites
friend un(e) ami(e)/un
    copain (une copine)
frightening effrayant
frontier la frontière
fruit le fruit
  fruit juice le jus de fruit
fruiterer le marchand de
    fruits
frying pan la poêle
full (capacity) plein
  (= no vacancies)
    complet (complète)
full board la pension
    complète
fun fair la fête foraine
furnished meublé
furnishing l'ameublement
    (m)
fuse le plomb/le fusible

G
game le jeu
  games room la salle de
    jeux
gangster film un film de
    gangsters
garage le garage

garage mechanic le garagiste
garden le jardin
gas le gaz
gate/fence la barrière
gear la vitesse
general général
generally généralement/en général
gentle doux (-ce)
gentleman le monsieur (pl messieurs)
gently doucement
geography la géographie
German allemand
Germany l'Allemagne (f)
to get on together s'entendre
gift le cadeau
to gift-wrap faire un paquet-cadeau
gin le gin
girl la jeune fille
to give donner
to give back rendre
glass le verre
to raise one's glass (toast) lever son verre
glasses les lunettes (f)
glove le gant
to go aller
to go and fetch/go for aller chercher
to go and see aller voir
to go around with fréquenter
to go away s'en aller
to go camping faire du camping
to go down descendre
to go home/back rentrer
to go in entrer
to go out sortir
to go up monter
to go with accompagner
goal le but
gold l'or
made of gold en or
golf course le terrain de golf
good bon(ne)
(at a subject) fort

goodbye au revoir
goodness! tiens!/mon Dieu!
gramme le gramme
grandchild le petit-enfant (pl petits-enfants)
granddaughter la petite-fille
grandfather le grand-père
grandmother la grand-mère
grandparent le grand-parent
grandson le petit-fils
grape le raisin
grapefruit le pamplemousse
grass l'herbe (f)
Great Britain la Grande-Bretagne
green vert
Green Card la carte verte
greengrocer le marchand de légumes
grey gris
grocer un épicier
grocer's une alimentation/ une épicerie
ground le terrain
on the ground par terre
ground floor le rez-de-chaussée
group le groupe
to guarantee garantir
guarantee le bon de garantie
guide le guide
guilty coupable
gust le coup de vent
gym/PE la gym
PE room la salle de gym
gymnastics la gymnastique

H
hair les cheveux (m)
hairdresser le coiffeur/la coiffeuse
half demi/la moitié
half-board la demi-pension
half-time la mi-temps
hall le vestibule
town hall un hôtel de ville
ham le jambon
hand la main

handbag le sac à main
handkerchief le mouchoir
to hang up
  (phone) raccrocher
haricot beans les haricots
  (m)
hat le chapeau
to have avoir
to have to devoir
  I have to je dois
head la tête
headlight le phare
health la santé
  good health/cheers! à la
    tienne/à la vôtre!
to hear entendre
heart le coeur
  heart attack la crise
    cardiaque
heat la chaleur
heating le chauffage
heatwave la vague de
  chaleur
to heel (a shoe) remettre un
  talon à
hello! bonjour!
  (on the 'phone) allô!
to help secourir/aider
help! au secours!
here ici
here is/here are voici
herring un hareng
hi! salut!
highway code le code de la
  route
hike/ramble la randonnée
to hire louer
hiring la location
to hitchhike faire de
  l'autostop
hobby le passe-temps/le
  hobby
hockey le hockey
hole le trou
hold the line! ne quittez
  pas!
holiday (vacation) les
  vacances (f)
Holland la Hollande/les
  Pays-Bas (m)
to hope espérer
horse le cheval

hospital un hôpital
hostess une hôtesse
  air hostess une hôtesse de
    l'air
hot chaud
hotel un hôtel
hour une heure
house/home la maison/le
  domicile
  at my house chez moi
hovercraft un aéroglisseur
how comment
  how do I get to . . .? pour
    aller à . . .?
  how long?
    (time) combien de
    temps?
  how much? combien?
  how much is it? c'est
    combien?
hunger la faim
  I am hungry j'ai faim
hurt blessé
husband le mari
hypermarket un
  hypermarché

I
ice/ice cream la glace
identification la pièce
  d'identité
identity une identité
if si
ill malade
illegal illégal
immediately immédiateme-
  nt/tout de suite
important important
impossible impossible
in dans/en
included compris
indicator le clignotant
information les
  renseignements (m)
information bureau le
  bureau de
  renseignements/le
  syndicat d'initiative
injection la piqûre
insect un insecte
inspector (train) le
  contrôleur

in dans
instead of au lieu de
insurance l'assurance (f)
insured assuré
to intend avoir l'intention
(de)
interesting intéressant
international international
interval un entracte
intolerable inadmissible
to introduce présenter
may I introduce je te/vous
présente
invitation une invitation
Ireland l'Irlande (f)
Northern
Ireland l'Irlande du
Nord
Irish irlandais
island une île
isn't it? n'est-ce pas?
Italian italien (italienne)

J
jacket la veste/le blouson
jam la confiture
January janvier
jar le pot
jeans le jean
jersey le tricot
jobless au chômage
joiner/carpenter le
menuisier
journalist le/la journaliste
journey le voyage
have a good journey! bon
voyage!
jug le pichet/la carafe
juice le jus
July juillet
jumper le tricot/le pull
June juin

K
to keep garder
key la clé
kilo le kilo
kind aimable
to kiss embrasser
kitchen la cuisine
knife le couteau
knob le bouton

to knock frapper
to knock down/
over renverser
to know (a
person) connaître
(a fact) savoir

L
ladder une échelle
lady la dame
lager la bière blonde
lake le lac
lamb un agneau
lamp la lampe
language la langue
large grand
last dernier (-ère)
at last enfin
late tard/en retard
later tout à l'heure/plus tard
launderette la laverie
automatique
lavatory le WC/le cabinet
de toilette
leaflet/folder le dépliant
leather le cuir
made of leather en cuir
to leave quitter/partir
left gauche
on the left à gauche
leg la jambe
leisure le loisir
leisure-time activities les
loisirs (m)
lemon le citron
lemon juice le jus de
citron
lemonade la limonade
to lend prêter
length (of time) la durée
less moins
a little less un peu moins
to let laisser
letter la lettre
letter box la boîte aux
lettres
lettuce la salade
library la bibliothèque
licence la licence
driving licence le permis
de conduire
lift un ascenseur

lift pass le forfait
to lift the receiver décrocher le combiné
to light allumer
light (weight) léger
  (colour) clair
light la lumière/la lampe
  (car) le phare
  dipped headlights les feux de croisement
  headlights les feux de route
  rear lights les feux arrière
  red light le feu rouge
  side lights les feux de position
  traffic light le feu
lighter le briquet
to like aimer
  I'd like je voudrais/ j'aimerais
lilo le matelas pneumatique
line la ligne
list la liste
litre le litre
little petit
  a little un peu
to live demeurer/habiter/ vivre/résider
liver le foie
loaf le pain/la baguette
to loathe avoir horreur de
lobster le homard
to lock fermer à clef
London Londres
long long
  a long time longtemps
to look (at) regarder
  (for) chercher
lorry le camion
  heavy goods vehicle le poids lourd
to lose perdre
lost property office le bureau des objets trouvés
lot
  a lot (of) beaucoup (de)
love l'amour (m)
  in love amoureux (-euse)
lovely beau (belle)/ravissant
lozenge la pastille

luck la chance
  good luck! bonne chance!
luggage les bagages (m)
  left-luggage locker la consigne automatique
luggage rack le filet
lunch le déjeuner
  to have lunch déjeuner
luxury de luxe

M
machine la machine
  washing machine la machine à laver
Madam Madame
magazine le magazine/la revue
  weekly magazine un hebdomadaire
mail le courrier
to make faire
make-up le maquillage
man un homme
manager le directeur
map la carte
  road map la carte routière
March mars
market le marché
married marié
to marry épouser/se marier avec
mashed (potatoes) pommes duchesse/pommes mousseline
match une allumette
  boxing match le match de boxe
  football match le match de football
material/fabric une étoffe
May mai
mayonnaise la mayonnaise
meal le repas
  cooked meal le plat cuisiné
  ready-cooked meal le repas préparé
  enjoy your meal! bon appétit!
meat la viande

mechanic le mécanicien/la mécanicienne
garage mechanic/owner le garagiste
medicine la médecine/le médicament/le remède
Mediterranean Sea la Méditerranée
medium cooked (of meat) à point
meeting la conférence/la réunion/le rendez-vous
  to arrange a meeting with prendre rendez-vous avec
melon le melon
member le/la membre
to mend raccommoder/réparer
menu la carte/le menu
metal le métal
  made of metal en métal/de métal
midday midi
middle le milieu
  in the middle (of) au milieu (de)
midnight minuit
milk le lait
million le million
mineral water l'eau minérale
minute la minute
to miss manquer
Miss Mademoiselle
mistake une erreur
mixture (medicine) le sirop
modern moderne
moment un instant/un moment
Monday lundi
money l'argent (m)
  pocket money l'argent de poche
month le mois
monument le monument
moped la mobylette
more plus
  a little more un peu plus
morning le matin/la matinée
most of la plupart de

at the most au plus
mother la mère
mother-in-law la belle-mère
motorbike la moto/le vélomoteur
  by motorbike à (en) moto/à (en) vélomoteur
motor-cyclist le motocycliste
motorway une autoroute
mountain la montagne
mouth la bouche
much beaucoup
  how much? combien?
mum/mummy maman
municipal municipal
museum le musée
mushroom le champignon
music la musique
  pop music la musique pop
musical musical
mussels les moules (f)
mustard la moutarde

N
name le nom
  Christian/first name le prénom
narrow étroit
nationality la nationalité
  nationality plate la plaque de nationalité
near près de/proche
  near here près d'ici
necessary nécessaire
  it is necessary il faut
neck le cou
necklace le collier
to need avoir besoin de
  I need j'ai besoin de
needle une aiguille
nephew le neveu
net (price) net (nette)
  (for fish) le filet
never jamais
new nouveau (nouvelle)/neuf (neuve)
news les informations (f)/les actualités (f)
newspaper le journal

next (to) à côté (de)
  (in order) prochain
nice gentil (-ille)
niece la nièce
night la nuit
  goodnight! bonne nuit!
nil zéro
no non/pas (de)
noise le bruit
noodles les nouilles (f)
noon midi
Normandy la Normandie
north le nord
  North Sea la Mer du
    Nord
nose le nez
not pas (de)/ne . . . pas
not at all pas du tout
note le billet (de dix francs,
    etc)
nothing rien
to notice remarquer
November novembre
number le numéro
nurse un infirmier/une
    infirmière
nylon
  made of nylon en nylon

O
occupied occupé
October octobre
offence (against the
  law) une infraction
office le bureau
  foreign exchange office le
    bureau de change
  lost property office le
    bureau des objets
    trouvés
  ticket office le guichet
officer (policeman)
  Monsieur l'agent
oil l'huile (f)
OK d'accord/entendu
  it's OK ça va
  are you OK ça va?/ça
    colle?
old ancien (-enne)/vieux
  (vieille)
omelette une omelette

on sur
one-way sens unique
onion un oignon
open ouvert
  open on Mondays ouvert
    le lundi
opera un opéra
operation une opération
operator
  international operator le
    service international
opposite en face de/ci-
    contre
optician un opticien
or ou
orange une orange
  orange juice le jus
    d'orange
orangeade une orangeade/
    une orangina
orchestra un orchestre
to order commander
original original
  in the original
    language en version
      originale
outside dehors
overcoat le pardessus
overcooked trop cuit
to overtake dépasser
owner le propriétaire
  (of café) le patron
oysters les huîtres (f)

P
packet le paquet
pain la douleur
  to have a pain (in) avoir
    mal (à)
pair la paire
pal le copain (la copine)
pale pâle
pamphlet la brochure
pancake la crêpe
panties le slip
paper le papier
  writing paper le papier à
    lettres
  newspaper/magazine le
    journal
papers les papiers (m)
parcel le colis/le paquet

parent le parent
to park stationner/(se) garer
park le parc/le jardin public
  car park le parking/le stationnement
part
  spare part la pièce de rechange
  part-time à temps partiel
party la surprise-partie/la boum
to pass/spend (time) passer
passer-by le passant
passenger le passager
passport le passeport
pasta les pâtes (f)
pastille/lozenge la pastille
pastries la pâtisserie
pâté le pâté
path le chemin/le sentier
pavement le trottoir
to pay payer
  to pay back rembourser
paying (not free) payant
payment le règlement/le paiement
peach la pêche
pear la poire
peas les pois (m)
  garden peas les petits pois
pedestrian le piéton
pedestrian crossing le passage clouté
pencil le crayon
penfriend le/la correspondant(e)
penicillin la pénicilline
people les gens (m)
  a lot of people beaucoup de monde
pepper le poivre
peppery/spicy piquant
per par
  per day/person/night par jour/personne/nuit
perfect parfait
performance la séance
perfume le parfum
perfumery la parfumerie
period pains les règles (f) douloureuses
permanent permanent

permission la permission
person la personne
  per person par personne
personal personnel (-elle)
petrol l'essence (f)
  2/3-star/ standard l'ordinaire (m)
  4/5-star/top-grade le super
  petrol attendant le/la pompiste
  petrol station la station-service
to 'phone téléphoner
photo la photo
physics la physique
piano le piano
picnic le pique-nique
piece le morceau
pig le cochon
pill la pilule
pillow un oreiller
pilot le pilote
pineapple un ananas
pitch/ground le terrain
place un endroit/un lieu
  to take place avoir lieu
plaice le cabillaud
to plan arranger/prévoir
plan le plan
plane un avion
  by plane en avion/par avion
plant la plante
plaster le sparadrap
plastic
  made of plastic en plastique/de plastique
plate une assiette
platform le quai/la voie
to play jouer
  to play football jouer au football
  to play music jouer de la musique
  to play the piano jouer du piano
play la pièce de théâtre
pleasant agréable
please s'il te (vous) plaît
pleased content

plug (electricity) la prise (de courant)
   (water) le tampon
plum la prune
plumber le plombier
pocket la poche
to point out indiquer
police la police/la gendarmerie
   police station le commissariat/le poste de police/la gendarmerie
   police van le car de police
   policeman un agent de police/un gendarme
   policewoman la femme-agent de police
policy (life insurance) la police d'assurance
pop (music) le pop
pork le porc
   pork products la charcuterie
port le port
porter le porteur
possible possible
   is it possible? est-ce possible?
to post mettre à la poste/poster
post la poste/le courrier
   postal order le mandat postal
   postbox la boîte aux lettres
   postcard la carte postale
   postcode le code postal
   post office le bureau de poste/les PTT/les P et T
poster/notice une affiche
postman le facteur
potato la pomme de terre
poultry la volaille
pound la livre
   pound sterling la livre sterling
prawns les crevettes (roses) (f)/les langoustines (f)
to prefer préférer/aimer mieux

prescription une ordonnance
present le cadeau
pretty joli
price le prix
   maximum price le prix maximum
   minimum price le prix minimum
   price list le tarif
priority (to vehicles on the right) priorité à droite
   (over secondary roads) passage protégé
   to have priority avoir la priorité/avoir le droit (de passage)
private privé
   private hospital la clinique
profession le métier/la profession
programme le programme
   (on TV) une émission
Protestant protestant
pudding le dessert
to pull tirer
pullover le pull(over)
punctured crevé
purchase un achat
purse le porte-monnaie
to put mettre/poser
pyjamas un pyjama
Pyrenees les Pyrénées (f)

Q
quantity la quantité
quay le quai
queen la reine
question la question
quickly vite/rapidement
   too quickly trop vite
quiet calme

R
rabbit le lapin
racing
   horse racing les courses (f) de chevaux
   motor racing les courses (f) d'auto

153

radiator   le radiateur
radio   la radio
railway   le chemin de fer
   French Railway   lá SNCF
to rain   pleuvoir
   it's raining   il pleut
raincoat   un imperméable
rare   rare
   (of meat)   saignant
raspberry   la framboise
rate (of exchange)   le taux
   de change
   reduced rate   tarif réduit
razor   le rasoir
to read   lire
ready   prêt
rear   l'arrière (m)
   rear-view mirror   le
      rétroviseur
receipt   le reçu
receiver
   to lift the receiver
      décrocher le
      combiné
reception office   le bureau
   d'accueil
receptionist   la
   réceptionniste
to recommend
   recommander/conseiller
record   le disque
   record player   le tourne-
      disque/la platine
recreation   la distraction
rectangular   rectangulaire
red   rouge
reduction   la réduction
to refuse   refuser
region   la région
registration certificate   la
   carte d'immatriculation
registration number   le
   numéro
   d'immatriculation
registration plate   la plaque
   minéralogique
to regret/be sorry   regretter
regulations   le règlement
to remain   rester/demeurer
to rent/hire   louer
rent   le loyer
renting/hiring   la location

to repair   réparer
repair   la réparation
   repair kit   la trousse de
      réparation
to repeat   répéter
   will you repeat that
      voulez-vouz répéter ça?
      répéter ça?
reply   la réponse
report (on an accident)   le
   constat
to reserve   réserver
reservation   la réservation
to rest   se reposer
rest (remainder)   le reste
restaurant   le restaurant
to return   retourner
return (ticket)   un aller-
   retour
Rhine   le Rhin
rib   la côte
rice   le riz
ride   la randonnée
right
   to have a right   avoir le
      droit
   you are right   vous avez
      raison
   on the right   à droite
   just right   à point
   (= not wrong)   correct,
      juste
to ring   sonner
ring   un anneau/une bague
ripe   mûr
   nicely ripe   à point
road   la route/le chemin
   trunk road   la route
      nationale/la grande
      route
roadway   la chaussée
roadworks   les travaux (m)
roast   rôti
roll   le petit pain
romance (film, book)   un
   film/un livre d'amour
roof   le toit
room   la pièce/la salle
   waiting room   la salle
      d'attente
rope   la corde
round   (adj)   rond

(around) autour (de)
all around tout autour
route un itinéraire
  bus route la ligne
    d'autobus
rowing boat la barque à
    rames
rucksack le sac à dos
rugby le rugby
rules le règlement
to run courir
to run over renverser/
    écraser
Russia la Russie
Russian russe

S
safety belt la ceinture de
    sécurité
sailboard la planche à voile
salad(s) les crudités (f)/la
    salade
salami le saucisson
sales les soldes (f)
  in a sale en solde
salesman/woman le
    vendeur/la vendeuse
salmon le saumon
salt le sel
salty salé
same même/pareil(le)
sand le sable
sandal la sandale
sandwich le sandwich
sardine la sardine
satisfied satisfait
Saturday samedi
saucer la soucoupe
sauerkraut la choucroûte
sausage le saucisson
to say dire
scampi les langoustines (f)
    frites
scene la vue
school une école
scooter (motor) le scooter
Scotland l'Ecosse (f)
Scottish écossais
screen un écran
screwdriver le tournevis

sea la mer
seafood les fruits (m) de
    mer
seasick
  I am seasick j'ai le mal de
    mer
seat le siège
seated assis
second deuxième
  second-class ticket une
    seconde
to see voir
see you! à tout à l'heure!
self-service store/
    restaurant le libre-
    service
to sell vendre
to send envoyer
separately à part/
    séparément
September septembre
serious grave/sérieux (-euse)
to serve servir
service (not)
    included service (non)
    compris
to set off partir
several plusieurs
sex le sexe
to feel shaky se sentir fragile
shampoo le shampooing
sharp pointu
sheep le mouton
sheet (bed) le drap
  (paper) la feuille
shirt la chemise
shivers des frissons (m)
shoe la chaussure
  shoe repairer's la
    cordonnerie
to shop/go shopping faire
    les courses
shop la boutique/le magasin
short court
shorts le short
to show montrer
show le spectacle
  film show la séance de
    cinéma
shower la douche
  to have a shower prendre
    une douche

155

shower block le bloc sanitaire
shrimps les crevettes grises
shutter le volet
sick malade
side la côté
to sign signer
silk la soie
  made of silk en soie
silver l'argent (m)
  made of silver en argent
since depuis
singer le chanteur/la chanteuse
single (ticket) un aller simple
sink un évier/un bac à vaisselle
sister la soeur
sit down! asseyez-vous!
size/waist la taille
  (for shoes/gloves) la pointure
skates les patins (m)
skating rink la patinoire
ski/skiing le ski
  ski-boots les chaussures (f) de ski
  ski equipment un équipement de ski
  skiing lesson la leçon de ski
  ski instructor le moniteur/la monitrice
  ski jumping le saut à skis
  ski lift le téléski/le télésiège
  ski pants le fuseau
  ski resort la station de ski
  ski run la piste
  ski slopes les pentes de ski
  ski sticks les bâtons de ski
  ski-touring le ski de randonnée
  ski tow le téléski
skirt la jupe
sledge la luge
to sleep dormir
sleeping bag le sac de couchage
slice la tranche

slim/slight mince
slot la fente
to slow down ralentir
slowly lentement
small petit
smart chic
smell une odeur
to smoke fumer
  (no-) smoking (non-) fumeur
snack bar le snack
soap le savon
society la société
sock la chaussette
socket la prise (de courant)
sole (fish) la sole
  (on shoe) la semelle
to sole a shoe ressemeler un soulier
son le fils
song la chanson
soon bientôt
  see you soon! à bientôt!
sorry! pardon!/excusez-moi!
I'm sorry je m'excuse/je suis désolé
Sound and Light (spectacle) son et lumière
soup le potage/la soupe
south le sud
souvenir le souvenir
Spain l'Espagne (m)
Spanish espagnol
spare parts les pièces de rechange
to speak parler
speciality la spécialité
spectacles les lunettes (f)
speed la vitesse
  speed limit la limitation de vitesse
to spell épeler
to spend (time) passer
  (money) dépenser
spicy piquant
spinach les épinards (m)
spoon la cuiller
  coffee spoon la cuiller à café
spoonful la cuillerée

sport   le sport
  sports facilities   les
      équipements (m)
      sportifs
  winter sports   les sports
      d'hiver
spouse   un époux/une
      épouse
to sprain (one's ankle)   se
      fouler (la cheville)
spring   le printemps
  in spring   au printemps
square   la place
  (adj)   carré
stadium   le stade
staircase   un escalier
stalls   le parterre/l'orchestre
      (m)
stamp   le timbre
  a one-franc stamp   un
      timbre à un franc
star (of film)   la vedette
to start   commencer
  (car engine)   démarrer
station   la gare
  (Metro)   la station
to stay   rester
stay   le séjour
steak   le steak/le biftek
  steak and chips   steak-
      frites
to steal   voler
steam   la vapeur
steering wheel   le volant
stepfather   le beau-père
stick   le bâton
  French stick (thick)   la
      baguette
  (thin)   la ficelle
to sting   piquer
stockings   les bas
stomach   le ventre/l'estomac
      (m)
to stop   arrêter/s'arrêter
store   le dépôt
stove   le poêle
  oil (paraffin) stove   le
      poêle à mazout (à
      pétrole)
strawberry   la fraise
street   la rue
string   la ficelle

strong   fort
student   un(e) étudiant(e)
sub-title   le sous-titre
suburbs   la banlieue
sugar   le sucre
suitcase   la valise
summer   l'été (m)
  in summer   en été
sun   le soleil
  sunburn   un coup de soleil
Sunday   dimanche
sunstroke   une insolation/un
      coup de soleil
supermarket   le
      supermarché
supplement   le supplément
supplementary   supplément-
      aire
sure   sûr
surf board   la planche de
      surf
sweater   le tricot/le pull
sweet   le bonbon
sweet   doux (douce)
  (= sweetened)   sucré
sweet shop   la confiserie
sweetcorn   le maïs
to swim   nager
swimming   la natation
  **swimming pool
      (outdoor)**   la piscine
      en plein air
  **swimming pool
      (indoor)**   la piscine
      couverte
  **swimming pool
      (heated)**   la piscine
      chauffée
  swimsuit   le maillot de
      bain
  swimming trunks   le
      maillot de bain
Swiss   suisse
switch   un interrupteur
Switzerland   la Suisse
syrup/mixture   le sirop
  cough mixture   le sirop
      contre la toux

T
table   la table

tablet/pill le cachet/le comprimé
to take prendre
taken (of seat) occupé
take-away à emporter
tap (faucet) le robinet/la prise d'eau
tart la tarte
taxi le taxi
  by taxi en taxi
  taxi rank la station de taxis
tea le thé
teenager un(e) adolescent(e)
tee-shirt le tee-shirt
to telephone téléphoner
telephone le téléphone
  telephone box la cabine téléphonique
  telephone call le coup de téléphone/le coup de fil
  telephone directory un annuaire
television la télévision/la télé
telex le télex
to tell dire
temperature
  I have a temperature j'ai de la température/de la fièvre
ten dix
tennis
  to play tennis jouer au tennis
  table tennis le tennis de table
  tennis courts les courts (m) de tennis
tent la tente
to thank remercier
  thank you very much merci bien/ beaucoup
that ça/cela
  that's (of price total) ça fait
  that way par là
theatre le théâtre
there y/là

there is/there are il y a/ voilà
thief le voleur
third troisième
thirst la soif
  I am thirsty j'ai soif
this ceci
thousand mille
thread le fil
throat la gorge
  I have a sore throat j'ai mal à la gorge
Thursday jeudi
ticket le billet
  ticket office le guichet
  ticket collector (at railway station) le contrôleur
tie la cravate
tights le collant
time le temps, la fois
  on time à temps/à l'heure
  a long time longtemps
  at what time? à quelle heure?
tin (of food) la boîte
  tin opener un ouvre-boîte
tip le pourboire
tired fatigué
tobacco le tabac
tobacconist's le bureau de tabac/le café/le tabac
today aujourd'hui
  today's special le plat du jour
together ensemble
toilet la toilette/le cabinet/le WC
token le jeton
toll (gate) le péage
tomato la tomate
tomorrow demain
tongue la langue
too (much) trop
tool un outil
tooth la dent
  toothache mal aux dents
  toothpaste le dentifrice/la pâte dentifrice
  to clean one's teeth se brosser les dents

toothbrush la brosse à dents
torch la lampe électrique
torn déchiré
total le montant/le total/la
    somme
towel la serviette
  hand towel un essuie-
    mains
  tea towel le torchon
town la ville
toy le jouet
track/platform la voie
traffic light le feu
tragedy la tragédie
train le train
  fast train un express
  non-stop or through
    train un train direct
  express train un rapide
  stopping train un
    omnibus
  high-speed train un TGV
  by train par le train/en
    train
transfer un virement
  to make a credit
    transfer faire un
    virement
tray le plateau
tree un arbre
trip une excursion
trousers (pants) le pantalon
trout la truite
true vrai
to try essayer
tube (of pills) le tube
  (the Underground) le
    Métro
  to go by tube prendre le
    Métro
Tuesday mardi
tuna le thon
turkey la dinde
to turn tourner
TV la télé
  TV news le télé-journal
twice deux fois
twin un jumeau/une jumelle
to twist tordre
two deux
  table for two table à deux

tyre le pneu
  burst tyre le pneu crevé
  spare tyre le pneu de
    rechange

U
umbrella le parapluie
uncle un oncle
under sous
underdone saignant
Underground le Métro
  by Underground en
    Métro
to understand comprendre
underpants le slip
underwear les sous-
    vêtements (m)
undrinkable (of water) non
    potable
United Kingdom le
    Royaume-Uni
university une université
unwell souffrant
urgent urgent
USA les Etats-Unis (m)
usherette une ouvreuse
useless inutile
usually généralement

V
vanilla la vanille
veal le veau
vegetable le légume
vehicle la voiture/le véhicule
very très
village le village
to visit visiter
visitor le visiteur/la visiteuse
to vomit vomir

W
waist la taille
to wait (for) attendre
waiting room la salle
    d'attente
waiter le garçon (de café)/le
    serveur
waitress la serveuse
Wales le Pays de Galles
to walk marcher

159

to go for a walk faire une promenade
walk la promenade/la randonnée
wallet le portefeuille
to want vouloir
warden le gardien
wardrobe une armoire
warning un avertissement
  warning sign un panneau avertisseur
to wash (se) laver
  to wash up faire la vaisselle
wash (e.g. car wash) le lavage
washbasin le lavabo
washroom les toilettes (f)
wasp la guêpe
watch la montre
water l'eau (f)
  water supply point la prise d'eau
to wear/carry porter
weather le temps
Wednesday mercredi
week la semaine
weekend le week-end
to weigh peser
well bien
Welsh gallois
west l'ouest (m)
western (film) le western
wet mouillé
what quoi/qu'est-ce que
wheel la roue
  spare wheel la roue de secours
  steering wheel le volant
when quand
where où
which quel(le)
whisky le whisky
white blanc (blanche)
Whitsuntide/Whit Sunday Pentecôte (f)
who qui
  who's speaking c'est de la part de qui?
whose/of which dont

why pourquoi
wide large
wife/woman la femme
window la fenêtre
  shop window la vitrine
windscreen le pare-brise
  windscreen wiper un essuie-glace
to win gagner
wine le vin (blanc/rouge/rosé/etc)
winter l'hiver (m)
  winter sports les sports d'hiver
to wish/want vouloir
with avec
without sans
woman la femme
wood le bois/la forêt
  made of wood en bois
wool la laine
  made of wool en laine
to work travailler
  (= to be in working order) marcher
  it's not working ça ne marche pas
worn/worn-out usé
to write écrire
  writing paper le papier à lettres
wrong faux
  to be wrong avoir tort

Y

year un an/une année
yellow jaune
yesterday hier
yoghourt le yaourt
young jeune
  youngest child le cadet/la cadette
youth hostel une auberge de jeunesse

Z

zero zéro
zone le zone
zoo le jardin zoologique/le zoo